It's about
Not
the
Horse

Other Hay House Titles
of Related Interest

Books

THE ANGEL BY MY SIDE,
by Mike Lingenfelter and David Frei

THE LOVE AND POWER JOURNAL, by Lynn V. Andrews

SIMPLE THINGS, by Jim Brickman

SIXTH SENSE, by Stuart Wilde

VISIONSEEKER, by Hank Wesselman, Ph.D.

Audio Programs

CHAKRA CLEARING, by Doreen Virtue, Ph.D.

INTUITIVE HEALING, by Judith Orloff, M.D.

THE MANIFESTATION PROCESS, by John Randolph Price

*THERE'S A SPIRITUAL SOLUTION
TO EVERY PROBLEM,* by Dr. Wayne W. Dyer

Card Decks

IF LIFE IS A GAME, THESE ARE THE RULES CARDS,
by Chérie Carter-Scott, Ph.D.

SELF-CARE CARDS, by Cheryl Richardson

WISDOM CARDS, by Louise L. Hay

ZEN CARDS, by Daniel Levin

All of the above are available at your local bookstore,
or may be ordered through Hay House, Inc.:

(800) 654-5126 or (760) 431-7695
(800) 650-5115 (fax) or (760) 431-6948 (fax)
www.hayhouse.com

It's Not about the Horse

It's about Overcoming Fear and Self-doubt

Wyatt Webb
with Cindy Pearlman

HAY HOUSE, INC.
Carlsbad, California
London • Sydney • Johannesburg
Vancouver • Hong Kong • New Delhi

Published and distributed in the United States by: Hay House, Inc.: www.hay-house.com • *Published and distributed in Australia by:* Hay House Australia Pty. Ltd.: www.hayhouse.com.au • *Published and distributed in the United Kingdom by:* Hay House UK, Ltd.: www.hayhouse.co.uk • *Published and distributed in the Republic of South Africa by:* Hay House SA (Pty), Ltd.: orders@psdprom.co.za • www.hayhouse.co.za • *Distributed in Canada by:* Raincoast: www.raincoast.com • *Published in India by:* Hay House Publishers India: www.hayhouse.co.in

Editorial supervision: Jill Kramer • *Design:* Ashley Brown
Interior photos: Photo of Wyatt Webb and Monsoon the horse:
   Courtesy of Mary Henebry

Library of Congress Cataloging-in-Publication Data

Webb, Wyatt.
   It's not about the horse-it's about overcoming fear and self-doubt / Wyatt Webb, with Cindy Pearlman.
      p. cm.
   ISBN 1-56170-978-6 (hardcover) • 1-4019-0128-X (tradepaper)
   1. Horsemanship—Therapeutic use. 2. Psychotherapy. 3. Horses—Psychological aspects.
4. Human-animal relationships. I. Pearlman, Cindy. II. Title.

RC489.H67 W43 2002
616.89'165—dc21

                                   2002001161

ISBN 13: 978-1-4019-0128-8
ISBN 10: 1-4019-0128-X

10 09 08 07   9 8 7 6
1st printing, August 2002
6th printing, May 2007

Printed in the United States of America

ↄↄ ↄↄ ↄↄ

This book is dedicated to Carin.

ↄↄ ↄↄ ↄↄ

Contents

PART I:
THE DREAM (a.k.a. "The Nightmare")

PART II:
WAKING UP (a.k.a. "Reality")

Foreword

by Cindy Pearlman

I came to Wyatt Webb with only one rule: He was not going to make me cry.

That seemed like an easy one. We were going to meet in Tucson, Arizona, where I would participate in the Equine Experience—and Wyatt would decide if I was the type of person who could help him write his story.

That decision would partly be based on what I could tell him about my own life. "No offense," he said when we first spoke on the phone, "but I don't want anyone helping me write this book who hasn't lived some."

In fact, that's about all he said. Oh, there was one more thing: "By the way, don't wear sandals. You'll be around horses." Click.

On the plane ride from Chicago, I sat crammed into an airplane seat in my new black suede desert boots and decided exactly how it would go with

Wyatt. I would tell him about a few of my minor struggles. I'd brush a horse. I'd probably get a nice tan. And we would size each other up—the no-nonsense therapist and the tough, big-city journalist.

About 45 minutes into my second day with Wyatt, the tears were rolling down my cheeks.

The day began with another type of waterworks threat, though, and that came from the storm clouds brewing over the mountains in Tucson. There I sat on hay bales with six other women, listening to Wyatt talk about the Equine Experience. Then we were told to go into the arena (a big, dusty area surrounded by metal fences) and choose our horses. I wound up with an 1,100-pound dark brown horse named Adieu who sized me up by craning his neck and glaring at me with an eyeball the size of a small lemon.

Wyatt had instructed us to greet the massive animals and then lift their extremely huge hooves, where we would use a picklike device to clean their shoes. *Was he nuts?* I thought, consoling myself with the fact that dogs love me, cats love me, and horses were just . . . bigger beasts who would certainly know that I was an animal person and thus listen to me. Of course, Adieu could have cared less about my qualifications. He wouldn't lift his foot for anything. "Squeeze the tendon at the bottom of his leg," Wyatt said, breezing by on his way to check on another guest.

I tried squeezing with both hands at one point.

I even broke a nail. Nothing. What to do? Since Wyatt was busy with the other women, and since Adieu probably had clean enough feet, I moved on to the third task, which was to brush the horse. Problem solved.

That's when I felt Wyatt standing close behind me as horse dust swirled around us. "So, you just skip over what's hard in life?" he said.

Bull's-eye! I'm busted! It was like being shot. Then Wyatt moved in closer, and in the most soothing, quiet voice that I have ever heard in my life, he whispered, "I can see that you're in a world of pain."

I could feel my bottom lip tremble, which mortified me. After a silent prayer that somehow a UFO would land and divert Wyatt's attention, I began to feel the tears well up in my eyes. Soon, they were sliding down my cheeks. My world of pain actually had to do with a traumatic romantic breakup. Suddenly, I was telling Wyatt all about it. I told him about how my ex continued to call about work projects as if there had been no other connection between us.

In true Wyatt style, which I've seen numerous times since that day, he sized up the situation in about 30 seconds. "I see you have a cell phone in your bag that's by the barn," he said. "Would you be willing to call that man right now and tell him . . . well, what do you *want* to tell him?" Wyatt never exactly tells you what to do. He likes you to figure it out for yourself.

"I want to tell him . . . ," I sobbed, "I—I want to tell him to fuck off!" Then I stopped cold, thinking that Wyatt would be sort of mortified that I wasn't only crying, but now I was also swearing. (Later, I would learn that the f-word is one of Wyatt's favorites.) "We're not calling this man to change his behavior," Wyatt said. "We're just letting you get something off your chest that's been sitting there like a bulldozer."

I made the call. He wasn't home, but I left a message. Mission accomplished in more ways than one. It was an ending to one part of my life—thanks to Adieu, the appropriately named horse. And it was a beginning to another part of my life, which was writing this book with Wyatt. (By the way, after making that phone call, my energy was suddenly unblocked, and the horse lifted his hoof in two seconds. When Wyatt turned away, I asked the horse for his hoof again, and with his back to us the entire time, Wyatt walked away, muttering, "So you don't believe that it works, huh?")

I've cried many other times in front of Wyatt Webb, and also behind his back while writing this book. I teared up while writing about his extremely tough childhood. I barely held back the tears when he told me about his descent into the depths of drugs and alcohol. I misted up several times when he talked about the people he'd met in rehab who saved his life. And on the Monday night at approximately 9 P.M. last winter when we wrote the last sentence of this book, I burst into tears like that day in the arena.

Let me make one thing clear: My tears were not out of sadness. Rather, they were tears of admiration for someone who descended into his own private hell and came out on the other side . . . which should be enough. But this is a person who took his second chance and used it for the greater good, and I'm proud to call him my partner on this project. I'm even prouder now to call him my friend.

On September 11, when the world was in chaos, I read one of the last chapters in this book again, where Wyatt talks about noticing the brilliant smile of a checkout girl at his neighborhood supermarket and speaking with the homeless guy who plays guitar outside the local Walgreens. Wyatt mentions worldwide prayer meetings and how the life force and energy of good can triumph over all that is harmful. I cannot think of a better time in history for people to hear that message.

Right about now, Wyatt probably will want to kill me for painting him as some saint. Okay, enough. Here's a bit of the lighter side of our collaboration. You see, when you work on a book with someone like Wyatt, you can just inject your daily concerns into the process from time to time. It's great free therapy—and just a phone call away. When you're blue, there's nothing better than hearing Wyatt's Southern drawl tell you, "Have a large day." (He also sometimes screens my potential dates.)

By the way, Wyatt is always right about that kind of stuff.

The other day I reminded him about the first time we met.

"God, I really lost it," I told him.

"No, you really found it," he said. "Do you get it?"

Wyatt, I finally do.

Preface

Welcome to Miraval
Life in Balance ™

*I*f *you want to deal with your demons, it's appropri-ate to make a pit stop at a place as hot as hell—Tucson, Arizona, in the summertime. It's 100-plus degrees right now—with dark, ominous clouds erasing the Santa Catalina mountaintops in the distance. It's the monsoon season, which means big storms. But for the five women and two men sitting on hay bales in front of Wyatt Webb, it appears that there are bigger storms brewing.*

A sweet, musty smell of horse lingers in the air, and for no reason at all, a 1,300-pound chestnut gelding fit-tingly named Monsoon rears and tears off in a farting, sweating gallop. This is his way of welcoming people to a new form of therapy that blends horse sense with common sense. Monsoon's massive body and thick mane and tail fly through the air as he releases a high-pitched scream that rips into your eardrums and rattles your insides.

Wyatt's just as much in awe of this beautiful animal

as everybody else is. He tells the group, "That's sheer joy. It's also an emotion that's somewhat foreign to most of us humans on a daily basis."

Perhaps it's time for an introduction.

"My name is Wyatt," he says to the seven people in front of him. "Welcome to the Equine Experience."

By the looks on their faces, these people are ready for an experience. They don't appear to have felt joy for some time. But they miss the feeling, so that's why they're here. They could clearly be elsewhere, but they chose the Equine Experience, which is offered every day of the year at Miraval, one of the top resorts in the world. Even though the people gathered in front of Wyatt certainly have the means to be doing something else at this particular point in time, they wouldn't prefer a seat in first class, or a velvet-covered cushion in the lobby of the Four Seasons—they're right where they belong.

Wyatt starts the session by telling these folks that he's not here to change anybody's life. "I don't have the power to do so," he says. "I don't have your answers. To allow you to think that I do would be a complete lie and a total disservice to you.

"Now I'm certainly not here to argue with or discredit traditional therapeutic modalities. I'm not accusing anybody of doing a shitty job or saying that traditional psychotherapy isn't helpful. But I certainly hope that we can add to whatever already exists in the therapy world as you know it."

Wyatt then shares with them what was told to him by Logan, the counselor who, 22 years ago, helped save his life, his mind, and his very soul (more about him later). What he said was this: "If you're to achieve the peace, joy, and spiritual fulfillment that you want so badly, it depends upon one thing and one thing only—your willingness to simply do something different."

So to those clients who have spent half a lifetime in therapy with minimal results, Wyatt smiles and states the obvious: "If the practice that you've been involved with hasn't produced definitive changes, then guess what? It's not working. Maybe what you're doing could be remedied so that you can discover what does work."

Now, even though Wyatt has been a practicing therapist for a number of years, his tools don't involve a leather couch and his helpers don't arrive in suits or high heels. Of course, they wear shoes—but not the kind they sell at Bloomingdale's.

"You're going to clean some hooves," he tells the group, "and you're going to groom the horse. How you relate to this animal will tell us what you've learned over the course of your lifetime concerning how you relate to all living things. Your basic training has come from learning how to treat people." He pauses and adds, "Remember one thing: It's not about the horse. I mean, sure, I can teach you a few basic skills that will keep you safe in any barn in the world, but what we're here to look at is what you've learned over the course of

your lifetime that either works for or against you in your relationships."

He stops for a second and then continues. "Keep in mind that you've been conditioned to be externally focused in all of your relationships. This is one of the true impediments to our being able to learn anything about ourselves. Let me ask you this: How much time do you spend during the day wondering what others are thinking and feeling, and concocting stories about why they're behaving as they do? See, as long as I'm focused on you in such a manner, it will be impossible for me to connect with you because I'm not present with myself.

"So, what I suggest you do is pay attention to what you're thinking and pay attention to what you're feeling. Know that these two things dictate the way you live your life. By focusing your attention internally as opposed to externally, you'll be able to be present enough to connect with any other living thing, which will also cause you to take responsibility for your life and how you live it. Will I judge you? Of course not! But I will observe."

Wyatt promises these people that today he will pay attention. "Ask me for help if you need it," he tells them. "I pledge to tell you the truth, to be kind, but sometimes to be blunt. Together, let's examine the stories you're making up to see how many of them are based in reality. Personally, prior to the age of 36, almost every story I had was based in a lie. But I'd like you to remember that it doesn't take nearly as many words to tell the truth as it does to bullshit somebody."

Here he switches gears, for it's time for a few specifics. "*The horses are the same for every person who chooses to be with them. Whichever horse you choose will serve as a mirror to your energy system— what you think, what you feel, and every move your body does or doesn't make."*

He makes it clear that the person dealing with the horse is the one who tells the whole story. And most of the stories he sees have one thing in common: pain. Most of this pain is rooted in self-doubt and fear. For instance, one man in the group says, "*I can't remember when I didn't hurt. I think it's the world that messes us up."*

"*Well," Wyatt asks him, "whose job is it to clean up the mess?"*

Then he turns to the audience and says, "*We've been imprinted. We're born being called 'bundles of joy.' Well, that's true. Babies generally* are *full of joy— they're born happy and remain so unless they're hungry or experiencing some discomfort. Once that's alleviated, they're right back in the joy state. They're at one with everything when they arrive on the planet. They run on pure emotion.*

"*They don't know what it means to doubt themselves or to be afraid until about five days into the trip,* when they begin to soak up the energy of the adults," Wyatt says. "Then they feel the inconsistency. At this point in time, welcome to a world full of scary people.

"Every culture I've ever been subjected to appears to be frightened," he explains. "I've been working as a psychotherapist for 20 years, and if I could boil down every problem that ever walked through any office that I've occupied—and this includes when I've been alone in the office—every human being suffers from two things in varying degrees of intensity, two things that are taught to us. They're called self-doubt and fear.

"There's the fear of physical harm and of emotional harm. There's the fear of not being good enough. There's the constant fear of being discovered. In fact, I've done a lot of team building with corporate systems, and what do you think the one thing that CEOs, presidents, and vice presidents of companies don't want the people working for them to know? They don't want anyone to know that at any given moment they might not have all the answers. I've been privy to and a part of this phenomenon by watching people move through the world 'bluffing it.' It seems that the vast majority aren't aware of what they're doing."

Wyatt's next words take the concept to a deeper level. "Anyone who really wants to grow, expand, and know who they are has to travel uncharted territories all the time. So that kind of person has to live in a world of 'I don't know,' which is scary, but that's the *only place where you learn anything. What you always find on the opposite side of fear and self-doubt is joy. Joy is our birthright—we're born with it. But it gets taken away from us and we have to go back and reclaim it.*

"So, what we'll do today is not about discovering *who you are. It's about* remembering *who you are," he says. "End of story."*

Wyatt gives the group some things to think about. "Why do we continue to fight with each other? Thousands of years ago, we began with hand-to-hand combat. Then we picked up some stones, which was followed by the fashioning of weapons. Now we have the means to eradicate ourselves from the planet. We even have the audacity to call this 'progress,'" he says. "The problem is that we're afraid, and that's the reason we fight each other. We keep making it about other countries or religions, and it's not. Why can't we sit down and talk about what we're afraid of? We're afraid to tell the truth."

Wyatt shakes his head and mentions that Monsoon solidified this theory for him about a year ago. "One day I was riding him, and I was transitioning from the walk to the trot to the canter. It's called 'changing gaits.' The walk to the trot—no problem. But even after ten years of riding, the power of that canter still scares me. I tried to push Monsoon into a canter twice, and both times I miscued him. My fear had me off balance—literally and figuratively. So, I eased back to the trot, and I got frustrated. Like I had done 10,000 times before when things weren't going my way, the tail started wagging the dog, so to speak. I was the friggin' dog, and here we were in a mess again.

"I was about to move into a canter for the third time, and again I felt that I was off balance. This time, I was determined to win. I said, 'The hell with it,' and cued him anyway. Monsoon shifted his massive frame, and I felt his power ripple underneath me." Wyatt pauses and takes a look at his audience, who seems to have forgotten about the prickly hay bales or threatening storm clouds.

"I was so off that most of my weight shifted forward, which in the horse world is called 'throwing the horse on the forehand.' This was his cue to stop. And he did. I flew over his head about 20 feet onto the ground. If I hadn't had a helmet on, it would have killed me. I hit the ground with a bang! People heard it all the way back at the barn, some 40 yards away.

"Somehow in my daze, I managed to get up, checked to see if I was dead, and brushed the dirt and muck off. Meanwhile, Monsoon was looking at me as if to say: 'What the hell are you doing down there?'

"In that humiliating, spirit-crushing, bone-aching, ah-ha! moment, a lightbulb went off in my head. I thought to myself, I finally get it. Anytime I'm in a

relationship with any living thing and I have the need to win, the possibility for connection and closeness is over. *All I ever wanted was that closeness and connection. In fact, I think we're all homesick for it.*

"*At the time, I wish I'd just been able to get honest enough to back off and go, 'Wyatt, you're off balance. Pull up or you'll get hurt.' But do you think I could even go to that place? I had to damn near kill myself to figure it out. I had this lesson to learn, and my spirit was saying, 'Yes, it's going to be a tough one. So let's go.'*

"*Thankfully, my spirit also said, 'Put your helmet on, you damn fool, so you can live through it and then learn from it,"* Wyatt says.

He goes on to explain that he's never had that same issue with Monsoon ever again. "*I've had that problem with a few people,*" *Wyatt laughs,* "*but I've been able to reign it in because when I find myself trying to win, it's time to stop. Because somebody has to lose. This whole culture is set up this way. We've got to win, which means we're going to lose. It means that we cannot even hope to connect with each other.*" *As he gazes at the crowd of onlookers, it seems like they finally get it.*

For Wyatt, it's all about connection, and the first step to healing is connecting with a horse. Those who want to connect have issues that include mental, physical, and emotional abuse not limited to marriages on the rocks, parent-child relationships gone bad, and much worse concerns including rape and abandonment.

Now it's time to get to work. The group is brought into a large arena and each person is told to choose one of the six large, inquisitive horses waiting for them. Next to each animal is a small bucket with tools to clean their hooves, and various other grooming utensils associated with preparing a horse for saddling.

Wyatt tells everyone to approach their horse and greet the animal at its shoulder. He takes aside one young man and suggest that he stop rubbing the horse for dear life.

"Try to leave a little fur on the horse, because the sun is gonna come out and I don't want him to get burned," he says quietly to the young man. "You also don't need to sweet-talk him."

"I'm trying to get him to like me so he'll cooperate," says the man.

"So," Wyatt asks, "is this one of your learned behaviors? Is your motto: If I'm nice to you, then you must be nice to me back?"

"I guess I always try extra hard to get people to like me," says the young man. "I figure if I'm the nicest person in the whole room, people will have to be nice to me back."

"Let me suggest to you the fallacy behind that one," he explains. "You're not really being nice to anyone. You're being manipulative. You're only acting

nice in the hopes of preventing people from rejecting you. True kindness comes with no charge. Later on, the universe just pays you back."

The mini-dramas being played out on this sandy desert floor can easily become much more serious, though. For example, Katie, a young lawyer whose parents abandoned her and sent her to live in various foster homes, is afraid of her horse because she's scared to death of being rejected again.

"If you walk through your fear that something must be wrong with you, then what you always find on the other side is that there's nothing wrong with you. And there's nothing to be afraid of," he tells her.

"What happens then?" Katie asks, sobbing.

"When you get to that other side, there's only one thing waiting—joy."

Those wanting that feeling are looking for some help—and God, does Wyatt understand how they feel. After all, it's impossible for him to forget his very first client. This guy was the toughest bastard he's ever worked with, and he almost made Wyatt give up on everything.

That man was Wyatt himself. . . .

౭౷   ౭౷   ౭౷   ౭౷   ౭౷   ౭౷

11

Acknowledgments

To Cheryl Richardson, I am overwhelmed by your generosity and support for me as I began and completed this work. I deeply appreciate everything you've done, along with who you are as a person.

Thank you, Reid Tracy and Danny Levin of Hay House publishers, for providing the vehicle for this segment of the trip. Special thanks to Logan Morrell, who gave me the foundation for my life's work; and to Jonas Irbinkskas, who has taught me more about horses than I would have ever dreamed of knowing, while at the same time teaching me about life. It is truly a shame that everyone in the world doesn't get to spend at least five minutes with him.

Thank you, Bill O'Donnel, for hiring me and supporting me in my work then and now. To Bunny Blankman; Jim Moore; Brent Baum; Joseph Denucci (who can be both places at once); and Mark Lawless, my attorney. To Heartwind (I miss you), Vern, Whitney, Monsoon, Adieu, and every horse I've been blessed to be in the presence of. To every client over the past 20 years who trusted me with their stories and consistently provided me with proof of the existence of God.

When we completed the last line of this book, I knew at the core of who I am that it couldn't have been done with anyone but Cindy Pearlman. She provided the structure and selflessness so that this could truly be my book.

Introduction

Let me begin by making one thing clear: I'm not a horse whisperer. I don't even see myself as a horseman. To me, a horseman is somebody who has probably spent a lifetime (or more) in relationship with horses. He can teach you all the little subtleties that accompany communicating with and riding such powerful animals. And if you choose to listen, he can even tell you all of those magical things that go into being in a relationship with a horse.

That's not me.

I've spent the past 22 years attempting to awaken from a 36-year spiritual and emotional sleep. You could even call it a coma. The first part of this book deals with that long sleep—how it was induced, the nightmare that ensued, and the eventual need for a wake-up call.

Please know that this part of the book is not about blaming anything or anyone. It's primarily a look at a multigenerational legacy . . . or at some basic training that didn't serve me when I became an adult. In fact, this part of my life is actually what author Joseph Campbell referred to as "the hero's journey" (I'll talk more about this later). I hope that at least a portion of this very personal story will be something that you can also experience. After all, there is no one hero—we're *all* heroes. The hero's journey is the voyage from birth to death, with the ensuing awareness that the spirit lives on.

Now what the hell does this have to do with horses?

Well, let me assure you that 30 years ago, being drunk on the back of a horse, running into a tree limb, and breaking my nose gave me no indication that one day these wonderful animals would serve as my co-therapists, spiritual mirrors, and some of the best teachers I've ever encountered. That's where the second part of this book comes in. I'll give you firsthand examples of how these remarkable creatures have taught more to people than anyone could ever have imagined.

As for me, I've never been anywhere for the reason that I think I'm there. It's a damn good thing that I didn't get the chance to plan my life's journey by myself—I was truly too scared in the early part of my life to do anything but mess it up.

In fact, the first time I decided to learn how to properly (and soberly) ride a horse, I enlisted the help of a dressage master who, after hearing me bitch because the horse I was riding wouldn't cooperate, said something to me that I still quote to others every single day: *"Webb, it's not about the horse."*

That being said, as you read this book, you'll find that a horse can help people just like you find comfort, happiness, and themselves.

But no, it's not about the horse. It's about us.

And so, within these pages, I hope you'll find a common bond of struggle and solution that might let you know that you're not alone.

For years I thought I was the only one going through these types of struggles, and I was convinced that I was crazy. Standing here now on a crisp fall day in Tucson, Arizona—one of the most beautiful places on Earth—and watching three of the most stunning creatures I've ever seen simply be who they are, with their tails held high, nostrils flaring open, and running for no other reason than the sheer joy of how good it feels, I know that I'm not alone and never have been.

I'm still somewhat crazy, though. I guess some things never change.

∞ ∞ ∞ ∞ ∞ ∞

PART I

The Dream
(a.k.a. "The Nightmare")

Chapter 1

လၢလၢလ

My Name Is Wyatt . . .

My name is Wyatt, and I'm eight years old. I went to bed last night convinced that God was pissed off at me.

I was told this by my next-door neighbor. It's not a person, but a building. I live next to the Baptist church, where I'm told that I'm "everything that is nothing."

I'm told that I'm bad. I'm terrible. I'm a sinner. I'm a real loser. In other words, I'm doomed before I even get to the third grade.

ｃｓ ｃｓ ｃｓ

It took me several decades to find out that the above wasn't even close to being true. Horses helped me unravel the lie.

My story begins without anything that has hooves

or that could kick your butt with four different legs. In fact, the only horsepower I came in contact with on a regular basis was in my Daddy's DeSoto.

Let's start at the beginning. I was born in a rural town in the Deep South, in the state of Georgia. Picture a place with 250 people and one dirt road. There was the post office, two general stores, one small school, and five churches.

I was the youngest of two boys in my family. I probably wouldn't be writing this book if I'd been considered "the good one." I was what they called "an unhappy child." But deep down, I was extremely afraid and had the self-esteem of a snail. I was afraid of other kids. I was afraid of the night. I was afraid of God, storms, and my father. I wondered almost every day if I could even survive life itself.

I saw the men in my family as tough guys. Of course, later on, I would find out that they were also very scared little boys, but in grown men's skins. Their tears were probably as wet and desperate as my own, but you never would have guessed that this could be true by looking at them. You see, fear manifested itself as violence in my family. These men knew how to get *really* mad—not the type of anger where you scream or swear, but the type of rage that could actually kill someone.

I remember that my parents told me I had two great-uncles who did time in prison for murder. Both of these men were my father's uncles. One of them, Uncle Jim, drew a pistol and shot a man for insulting his wife. He supposedly went to jail for five years.

The other one, Uncle Perry, had "received word" that a man in his town had said that the next time he saw Perry, he was going to whip him. Well, one day, Uncle Perry was on his way to the cotton gin with his crop, and he put a nine-shot revolver under the seat of his horse-drawn wagon. When he arrived at the cotton gin, this man came out of nowhere and hit him with what's called "a single tree" (a heavy piece of equipment made of wood and metal that you put behind plow horses to keep the lines balanced).

This truly was a life-threatening blow. When the man hit Uncle Perry with this instrument, it knocked him off his wagon seat, but it didn't render him unconscious. When he came up out of the wagon, Uncle Perry had the revolver in his hand, and he shot the man nine times.

One shot probably would have stopped the attack. I think maybe the other eight shots are what sent him to prison.

Years after their prison stints, I met Uncle Perry and Uncle Jim, but I have no memory of them ever smiling. And so, the stories of men in my lineage did nothing but cause me to feel "different" because I wasn't tough like them.

What made it worse was that I was raised so close

to the aforementioned church. My mother was an organist and sang in the choir; and when I was five years old, my father had his religious conversion. From what I've heard about him prior to this conversion, it was his nature to be a hell-raiser, which is a trait I would echo myself in later years.

After his conversion, religion caused my father to become almost a stranger to me. He didn't seem to have much fun at all; in fact, most of the people I saw in our congregation seemed sad. They called themselves "good, God-fearing people." Therefore, being good and being fearful seemed synonymous to me. Later on, I found this to be an insane concept.

If you'd asked me at age eight to describe God, I would have said that He was 100 feet tall and had long white hair and a gray robe. He was looking down only at me, and His book was always open so He could keep score. As a result of what He saw with me, God was frowning.

It was almost like my being alive was a damn mistake.

For as long as I can remember, I had a basic belief that I was ugly. Very ugly. When I was a little boy, a neighbor lady came over to visit my mother, and they had no idea that I was in the house. I heard them talking to each other, and my mother told her the story of the first time she saw me.

Mom was in the recovery room with my father,

Marvin, and the nurse brought me in. "I will never forget the first time I saw Wyatt," my mother said to the neighbor. "They drew the covers back, I looked at him, and then I burst into tears. I said, 'Oh my God, Marvin. Isn't he ugly?'"

I snuck out of the house that day, feeling flawed and wartlike.

My brother, Jerome, who was five years older than me, had none of these problems. At least not that I could see. It wasn't his fault that my parents would often say to me, "Wyatt, why can't you be more like your brother?" The answer was simple: My brother was perfect. He was good-looking, a great athlete, and admired by everyone. I wanted to be just like him so that I would be admired, too.

I did have one thing going for me as a kid: I was damn funny. I got attention and positive strokes for "doing my act." This basically consisted of clowning around and doing fairly decent impersonations (for a prepubescent boy). I could do preachers, Jimmy Durante and other celebrities of the day, and some of the characters in my own hometown.

I also became aware that being the family clown had its drawbacks. On more than one occasion, I was asked to be quiet so I didn't embarrass the family. I was chided for talking too much. My brother would shake his head and say, "Your mouth is going to get you in big trouble one day."

Pretty interesting statement, because little did I know that one day I'd make a living with my mouth. For 15 years, I found success on stage as a professional singer and entertainer. And later, I'd discover the words that would stop me from killing myself with alcohol and drugs.

Eventually, I became a therapist, and I'd use my mouth to help stop other people from killing themselves. I'd speak to individuals from all walks of life about their problems. I'd talk to battered wives, rape victims, incest survivors, and people with wounds so deep that there didn't seem to be any way to ever heal them.

And the funny thing is that I'd do that at times standing next to a horse, a creature with a bigger mouth than I had, but who didn't say a word. But just like me, the horse had its own way of just not shutting up.

Chapter 2

CPCPCPCP

A Boy's Life

Maybe some people have had childhoods that are like Hallmark cards. But then there are those of us whose youth seems like it should have come with one of those Surgeon General's warnings: *Caution—growing up is hazardous to your mental health.*

Suffice it to say, my childhood was difficult for me, in spite of how hard everyone tried. I'm not blaming anybody—I'm just describing a legacy that was passed on to me and how that impacted who I am today. I know that now it appears that my life has turned out to be quite perfect thus far . . . but keep in mind that even good steel has to be passed through the baptism of fire.

One of the things I remember most about my childhood is my father leaving the house at the first hint of sunlight. He worked for Burlington Industries as a master mechanic, and from what I understand, he possessed skills that would have been close to those of a mechanical engineer. He only had a high school education, but he had innate abilities and worked his way up to an important job. Ultimately, he was put in charge of all the machinery at the largest cotton mill in the Burlington chain.

My father actually came to Georgia in the 1930s to play baseball. Dad came to the little town of Shannon, Georgia, when one of the mills recruited him as a ballplayer. Many of the small towns in the South at that time sponsored what they called "Mill Teams." They would actually give you a job, and then on weekends, you would don your uniform, grab your glove, and do what you were truly paid for—which was to compete in the Northwest Georgia Textile League.

As an aside, let me just say that when I was a kid, I knew more about baseball than anything else. And to this day, it's the only game that I miss playing.

Anyway, back to Dad. He was 28 years old when he met my mother, who was 18 at the time. They met while he was a patient in the hospital. He'd had a serious automobile accident, and a friend of my mother's invited her to go to the hospital because her boyfriend was a patient there. When my mother walked out of his hospital room that day, my dad found all the steely determination he could muster and announced to his sister, "That's the woman I'm going to marry."

He *did* marry her, three months later. At the time,

my father was making $12.87 a week. I remember him saying that from this whopping paycheck, five dollars would buy more groceries than he could carry. It also afforded my parents the luxury of paying the rent. And they were able to put some money away to build the house where I grew up, two doors down from the Baptist church. That house continues to exist to this day.

$$\mathcal{S} \quad \mathcal{S} \quad \mathcal{S}$$

My earliest memory of being on this earth is a little strange. I remember being five years old and feeling like one of those aliens that supposedly landed in Roswell, New Mexico. Even at that age, I felt like I was different from everyone around me, and I had serious doubts that I'd ever be able to fit in anywhere. I felt that there was something flawed about me—I didn't even fit in with my own family. Many times, I'd scan the dinner table as if I were taking things in with one of those slow-motion cameras.

I'd examine these faces that I saw every single day, and while their mouths were being stuffed with chicken and potatoes, I'd just think to myself, *I don't know who these people are. Am I like them? Am I really one of them?*

I didn't blame them for being the way they were in those days. I still don't. It wasn't about *them* at all.

There was just something amiss about the whole thing, like the rest of the world was 200 feet above me. I tried to be like them, I really did. I became very athletic, but as is the case with many families, it's the firstborn who's the father's child. I was afraid of my father, but oh, how I longed for his approval! The closest I could get to it was to be like my brother, who was very much like my father. My brother was almost like a conduit to my dad. He was like the burly bouncer who could either keep Daddy for himself or let me in every once in a while.

Meanwhile, I was Mama's favorite. My mother gave me the majority of her attention and would talk about me being "such a sweet child." She pretty much always thought that I was wonderful. But see, I don't think that either parent knew me—ever. Which is okay.

What wasn't okay was being a sensitive boy in the Deep South back in the 1940s. This story I'm about to tell will illustrate what I mean. When I was eight, I had two little Boston terriers named Popeye and Olive, whom we had raised from little pups. Popeye died of distemper, but my father sure tried to save that little dog's life. He tried medicine and vets and all the TLC in him because my father was a dog man. His nickname back then was "Big Dog" Webb because he always had a kennel full of high-quality hunting dogs. At the time, it appeared to be easier for him to dispense sensitivity and nurturing to his dogs rather than to his children or other humans.

Well, Olive had been in heat. A lot of dogs were trying to get at her, so we put her in my grandmother's shed. The door had a latch on it that wasn't really tight—at least that's what we thought. One day, I came home from school and found her dead. She had pushed her little head through the door, and the wood had choked the life out of her.

When I found her body, I began crying so hard that I could barely talk. That's how my father found me when he came home from work that afternoon.

My father took one look at my red, tear-stained face and asked, "Wyatt, what's wrong with you, boy?"

I couldn't speak. I just pointed at Olive's head. You see, I'd been pulling hard, but I couldn't get her head out of that door. In my child's mind, I didn't want her to hurt anymore, even though she'd been dead for some time. My dad opened the door for me and freed her body, and at that point, I could only think of one thing to do. I wanted to bury my dog in my own backyard where even in the winter the sun came down hard and warm. Instead, my father took Olive and put her in the trunk of his car. It was a cold winter day, and we drove out into the countryside. At one point, he stopped the car, got out, opened the trunk, and removed Olive's lifeless body. He tossed the carcass into some honeysuckle vines. I remember not saying a word, but I bit my lip hard so that I wouldn't cry again.

That night, I couldn't sleep because I knew my dog was cold. She was freezing and alone, and had been thrown away like the trash. Little did I know that like little Olive, my scars also wouldn't get their proper burial for many, many years.

*ﾟ   *ﾟ   *ﾟ

Maybe now it's time to reintroduce you to the Baptist church that was about 100 yards from my front door—a place that terrified me, shamed me, and eventually led me to look elsewhere for help and salvation.

This particular version of organized religion painted a rather dismal picture of the Deity. The overall message was that human beings weren't worthy of God's love. We were told repeatedly by the church's pastor, "You are here on Earth to suffer and do God's will."

I was never quite sure what the hell that was, to be honest.

And we were told, "In the end, if you behave correctly, your reward will be heaven. If you don't listen to what the church says, then the consequences will be a front-row seat in hell."

So, as you might imagine, I was very afraid of God. I also had a lot of questions that I couldn't really ask anyone. I had one, specifically: If God loved me so much, then how in the world could he ever let me go to this hell place? I thought, *For Christ's sake, is this my destiny?* Then my mind would race and think that mankind was surely much less evolved than God. And if God was this way, then I was for damn sure not safe down here with humans who were so much less evolved. I mean, if God wasn't safe, then mankind certainly wasn't either. How would I survive?

Later on, I read that Albert Einstein said, "There is only one question a human being really has to ask himself: 'Is the universe a safe place?'"

Was I scared for my life? You bet your ass I was. And then I slowly became afraid of *everything*. I was afraid of the dark. I was afraid of people who were older than I was. At four years old, I would look out my back window at the school I would attend someday, and I would watch all these kids play behind the building. I was terrified down to the core of my soul, and I said to myself, "I'll never be able to fit in," which pretty much became the story of my life.

I was too ugly. Too skinny. Too stupid. It just wasn't going to work for me. I sat with that, and I sat alone. Back then, there was no place to take those feelings. I couldn't tell anyone, for I knew that if I did, the response from my family would have been, "Wyatt, there's nothing to be afraid of, son." Yes there was. There was *everything* to be afraid of in those days.

Of course, I did go to school. I did the things all little boys did back then. I played baseball. I had friends. I didn't even get beaten up that much. My brother was such a tough guy that the word on the street was that you didn't mess with him or his family.

Sure, I got picked on some. When I was in the first grade, I used to fight with my buddy Billy Johnson. Nothing serious. We had little shoving matches. It was good for your reputation as a man, because even as a little guy, there was one thing you didn't want to be in the South: chickenshit.

So on the surface, I would shove and punch. Deep down, I felt compelled to do so—all the while hating every moment of it. Alas, I *was* chickenshit, but it didn't matter, because there's one truth we've seen over and over again on this planet: It's dangerous to mess with a scared person. So I made myself seem a little dangerous by feeling that danger inside that was really just rage boiling up in me. There were things I figured I was capable of doing, and frankly, they frightened me.

In the depths of my soul, I knew that I didn't want to be like the men in my family. They carried around a lot of shame and fear . . . and they were really dangerous. The way they dealt with their feelings is the way a lot of men cope with emotions. They *raged* their way out of it.

Of course, alcohol was another means of escape. Back then, there were no 12-step programs; they didn't even call it "alcoholism." If you had a problem with booze in the Deep South, people just said, "He was bad to drink." My mother's Uncle John? *He* was sometimes bad to drink.

From some of the stories I heard about him later in life, I see that my dad was most likely a problem drinker, but he stopped drinking prior to his religious conversion. My mother says that the last time she smelled alcohol on his breath was the day I was born. He celebrated me, and then he quit. Of course he was still scary at times, but at least he wasn't bad to drink.

Speaking of "scary," corporal punishment was an accepted form of child rearing in those days. Later on, therapists would tell me that I was a physically abused child. I didn't see it in those terms, and I still don't. We called it "getting a whipping." We'd screw up, and my father would line up my brother and me and pull off his belt.

I remember once I called my mother a son of a bitch. I got whipped three times that day. My brother whipped my ass; my mother went out and cut a switch and whipped my ass; then my father came home, and it was more of the same. I never called my mother a SOB—at least not audibly—ever again. Was I mad? Yes. But I learned how to internalize my rage quite proficiently.

౧౧ ౧౧ ౧౧

Around the time of my tenth birthday, it was suggested that it was time for me to be "saved." Getting saved was no easy deal. Basically, at the end of a lengthy sermon laced with hellfire and brimstone, the preacher gave what was known as the "altar calls." This basically amounted to inviting those who were convinced that they were hopeless without Jesus to get out of their church pew, come down to the altar, fall to their knees in front of it, and ask God to forgive them for their sins.

Now, you might ask, "Wyatt, what exactly *were* your big sins at age ten?" Well, it's rather simple. Cursing. Lying. Smoking. Stealing. Those were major sins, all of which I had committed, but none were as awful as masturbating. Oh, God! This was referred to a "the sin of onan" from the pulpit—as in "it's better to cast your seed onto the belly of a whore than onto the ground."

At the time, I was too young for whores. That only left the ground. So I was truly awful. See, I knew that anything that felt that good just had to be wrong. So said the preacher—a wiry little dark-haired man who yelled, screamed, and stomped around while he told you 101 reasons why you were going to a place someday that was comprised of eternal fire. Previously, I had experienced the pain of a burn on our stove, so this was some truly scary shit.

But back to the good stuff. This wasn't talked about openly, but it was understood that if you touched yourself, it was like the devil himself had possessed your hand and taken it to that nether region, which was previously reserved for your underwear and the family doc. Peeing, however, was acceptable.

Let's just say that I was a normal, curious little boy with a very active imagination. I always concluded my business with a visit with the Deity. When I was done, I'd feel extremely ashamed and guilty, and I would say to God, "Please forgive me. I'll never do it again." Imagine how horrible I felt when I couldn't keep that promise.

But there were far worse sins than a lust-filled mind. God, there were so many.

We were considered one of the more affluent families in the area, as we were the first ones to actually have a television. Well, everyone knew that TV was the work of the devil. Smoking cigarettes was the work of the devil. Dipping snuff—the devil strikes again! Movies were out of the question. Neither my father nor my mother ever went to a movie with us boys. It was against their religion.

Everything was a damned sin. In a nutshell, anything found standing outside of the "Baptist box" was bad for you. Anything that seemed to be any fun or that had any joy attached to it was bad for you. This is why you needed to be saved, but the funny thing was that later on, I would *really* need to be saved. And I would be so cynical about the whole idea of it that for years I put up walls of steel against the loving God who would eventually save my very life.

Anyway, my descent began at the age of 12 or 13. For one thing, I was what they might call "ahead of my time." I was drawn to the music of the black culture.

Prejudice ran rampant in the Deep South of the 1950s. I remember once asking my family why we didn't have any Negroes in our church. They looked at me like I was nuts and said, "Son, they have their own church-es." But their church was on the edge of town, because the great minds of the South at that time saw black people as being subservient. They weren't even second-class citizens—they were *fourth*-class citizens. I didn't understand this thinking because black people didn't seem as sad to me as most of the whites I knew. I wondered if their God was different from the one we had. Theirs seemed to bring more joy. And their music certainly had more pop to it than ours.

Meanwhile, I was growing up into a teenager who found little joy in my own life. I didn't even like Christmas: There was a buildup to it, and then it was over. I was depressed by the horrible letdown. In fact, I figured that most of life would be a horrible letdown if I stayed in this town. I knew I just *had* to get out of there. It certainly wasn't that I thought I was better than anyone else; I just needed to find someplace where I could fit in. I knew that Georgia wasn't it.

I wanted to see the world. To that end, I had two big

dreams: One was to play baseball for the New York Yankees, and the other was to be a movie star. Well, there were no movie studios at the time in Gordon County, Georgia. So I chose sports. Everybody wanted me to play football, and I did play one year as my school's quarterback, but I was terrified. Could I tell anybody? Of course not. I was determined that no one would ever discover that I was chickenshit. But inside my gut, in that spot where your stomach gives you a sort of internal forecast, I felt queasy. A terrible, cold voice told me that something was very, very wrong.

I masked it as best as I could. In fact, I hid quite a lot of things. I was a smart boy, but academically, I barely made it out of high school—I graduated with four D's, one C, and an F. The one saving grace is that I became such a good basketball player that I had six athletic scholarship offers, but my grade-point average was so horrible that I couldn't pass muster with the academic folks.

I was considered a glitch. I heard, "Wyatt, we want you to play ball, son, but there's no way they're going to admit you to this school." The coaches at the University of Kentucky and the University of Georgia tried to recruit me, but in the end, there was no scholarship for me.

I had already learned how to sabotage myself.

This was horrible, because remember how I wanted to be just like my brother, Jerome? Well, he was a big success. He got a scholarship to the University of Georgia to play football. Then he hurt his knee, but they just switched it to a baseball and basketball scholarship—he was that good of an athlete. He was also motivated to exceed expectations. For example, he went to New York City on his senior high school trip. He went to a place of worship that had more effect on our lives than any church, called Yankee Stadium. Well, my brother came back and carved 24 notches on his bed and boasted, "That's how old I'll be when I'm in the major leagues!"

True to form, Jerome dropped out of school at age 19 and was signed by the Cleveland Indians, for whom he played minor-league baseball for seven years. As always, I wanted to follow in his footsteps, so I said, "*I'm* going be a ballplayer. I'm going do it somehow, some way."

The biggest part of that dream was that I'd end up in the major leagues playing with my brother on the same team. But like most dreams, they end and you've got to wake up the next morning.

I remember the day my brother got released from the minors. I gazed out my bedroom window and saw him pull up in the driveway. I was 19 years old, and I saw failure. It hit me like a smack in the face. And I couldn't see his shame or feel his pain, although it registered in every crevice of his face. All I could think about was me. I said to myself, "What the hell am I supposed to do now?"

Chapter 3

❧❧❧

The Highs and Lows of My Music Career

When I was ten years old, my folks gave me a transistor radio. I would crawl under my covers when I was supposed to be asleep and listen to WLAC-AM, which came to me directly from Nashville, Tennessee, in all of its 50,000-watt, clear-channel glory.

As I mentioned before, I loved black music. So I'd clutch my radio and stay up way too late almost every night, listening to Muddy Waters, Bobby "Blue" Bland, Lightin' Hopkins, and countless others—and I'd dream of a way out of the funk that passed for my life.

When my brother left professional sports, I turned my back on it, too. I made a decision the day that Jerome threw a dose of reality at my baseball fantasy: I wasn't going to play ball anymore either. I was going to be a professional entertainer.

Of course, no one supported this decision, because at the time, I was already a sophomore at West Georgia College. I was leading the nation in small-college baseball stats—in batting average and stolen bases—and professional scouts were coming around to look at me. I was well on my way to joining my brother in playing pro baseball, but that little plan became moot.

I decided that I was going to set the world on fire as a singer. I had my eye on stardom, and I was going to become bigger than anyone could imagine. I wanted to hang gold records on the wall and tell the world to kiss my ass.

I'd always had a good singing voice, and I certainly felt that I had all of the makings of a superstar, but my musical beginnings were very humble. I started singing blues in the black clubs in Atlanta. We basically had six white guys playing rhythm and blues for a black audience in their nightspots on Auburn Avenue (which, coincidentally, was also the location of the famed Ebenezer Baptist Church where both Martin Luther Kings—senior and junior—were pastors).

On hot, sultry summer nights, the black musicians would nod to us and invite us onstage to join in. It wasn't about skin color—it was about the joy of the music and their generosity toward us. But it wasn't about money either. The most I could ever remember making was $32 in one night, which was actually considered a pretty good haul.

It was a beautiful thing to be accepted and praised on what they called "The Chitlin' Circuit." The people treated me wonderfully. I'll never forget Eddie Ellis, Arthur Connelly, and a beautiful black lady named Myra. She was the most graceful dancer I ever saw, even if she did always dance with her purse on her arm.

In those clubs, I learned that everything my town had taught me about race was absolutely wrong. The memories of that time in my life on Auburn Avenue are great ones, and they're all mine.

ᵔᴥᵔ ᵔᴥᵔ ᵔᴥᵔ

I also had a family to support during this time. You see, during my senior year in college, I got married; soon after that, our son, Jarrod, was born. I needed some steady work to support my new family, so I took a job as an assistant manager of a country club. There I was, dreaming of fame . . . and also trying to figure out what one should do as a husband and father.

One day I got a call from a friend of mine named Ken Vassey. He'd left Georgia behind and had gone to sunny California to make his mark on the world of big-time show business. Ken was one of the most talented people I'd ever met in my life. He could play anything that had keyboards or a string and could sing to the point of touching every corner of your soul. Eventually, after almost starving to death, he hooked up with a guy named Randy Sparks in Los Angeles, and they formed a band.

Ken went on to become a member of Kenny Rogers and the First Edition, and one day, I looked up and saw my old buddy on TV. He was performing on *The Tennessee Ernie Ford Show,* and I said to myself, "These guys are going to be stars."

I didn't waste much time making a decision that would almost kill me sooner rather than later—I called Ken, and he said, "Come out to L.A. I'll get you an audition with Randy."

Now keep in mind that I was 24 (a little old to get started as a rock star), and I already had a family. I was also overweight, not much of a looker, and didn't have the highest self-esteem that the world had ever seen. But I had a little friend to help me overcome all my insecurities. I met my pal in college, and we became very close, hooking up with each other as often as possible. My buddy was a drug commonly known as "speed."

I'm the guy who started drinking at age 15. Even though I puked my guts out the first time I tried hard liquor, practice made perfect, and soon drinking wasn't enough. I tried speed for the first time at age 17, and so began a 21-year addiction that incorporated both drugs and alcohol. I really wasn't too particular when it came to clouding my mind—whatever was handy would do.

Anyway, I mustered up the courage to fly out to L.A. for my audition, and I was flying in all sorts of other ways when I hit that stage in a little club called Leadbedders on Wilshire Boulevard. Leadbedders was owned by Ken's friend Randy Sparks, the man who signed Ken to a management contract and who had previously formed, recorded, and sold The New Christy Minstrels.

The place was packed to the rafters. And I was scared to death. Suddenly, I was that little alien boy from Georgia who didn't belong here, there, or anywhere. So I started this blues song off in the wrong key. The crowd began to squirm. I could see Randy looking down at his shoes. Finally, two songs later, I walked offstage to that mercy type of applause where people's hands are barely meeting each other.

I ran out the backstage door and punched a brick wall, breaking my hand. That was all I knew how to do. My shame hurt worse than the broken bones (but that was no picnic either).

Randy came outside and said, "You've got a pleasant talent, but you're never gonna make anybody believe you're 16 years old, and that's what I need."

Then he told me something I will never forget: "Wyatt, there are two kinds of people who make it in this business," he said. "There are the people who are totally gifted, like your friend Ken. And then there are people who are just damn persistent. You probably fall into the second category."

I was hurt deeply. So I just thought, *Fuck you, mister.* That was the way to react to your pain, right? Just get angry. I came back to Georgia like a bat out of hell. And then I suddenly became what Randy Sparks told me I was.

I took a wad of cash to the local record store, bought some Merle Haggard records, and started singing country music. See, country fans were loyal—they didn't care if you were old and fat and ugly, and so this was to be my door to filling the hole in my soul.

I got a record deal with a small label, and I moved my family to Nashville. I sent the first record I did to Randy Sparks. I don't know if he ever even listened to it, but if he did, I doubt he was impressed.

Five records and fifteen years in the music business followed. I worked clubs 30 weeks a year, and it was work that nearly killed me. I got to the point where I was too sick to sleep—but I was smarter than my own body, which was screaming for medical help and rest. So I deepened my relationship with chemicals, and this time I fell madly in love with uppers. They helped me stay up all night. They lifted my spirits. I was no longer below everyone else—I was on the same level.

In my haze, I thought I'd found the solution I'd been looking for my entire life. And I came to realize later that my addictive process was nothing but a spiritual quest. Well, let me tell you that when I go on a quest, it's really a quest. It's not for sissies.

One night I was playing at a club in Colorado, and in the bar after the show, I counted 67 different liquor bottles stacked up on those tantalizingly well-lit shelves. I bragged that I had drunk every one of those 67 brands at one time or another. Hell, I didn't discriminate when it came to getting high—anything that swirled or slid down my throat got my version of a welcome mat.

The pills brought me up, and the liquor evened out the feeling. I wasn't below or even level with the world anymore. I was flying. I was finally above everyone else, and I had no intention of ever coming down. And you know what? If that mixture of chemicals had continued to have the same effect, I'd either still be doing it now or I'd be dead—probably the latter. But, as most addicts eventually come to find out, I learned that as high as the drugs took me, they dropped me even lower.

This was my way of life for *21 years:* Highs so high I was a human F-16, and lows so low I didn't need a funeral because I'd already buried myself.

I got away with it for years. But there were major consequences that I chose to deny. For instance, when I was 30, I blew the opportunity to get a big-time recording contract with a major label. See, there was a guy named Larry Butler whom I met when he was a session musician. He played piano during one of my recording sessions and later was hired as a record producer at Capitol Records in Nashville. He'd told me prior to taking the position that he was impressed with my talent and believed we could cut hit records together.

When he got the job, I called him. He said, "Wyatt, I'd love to record you, but you have to wait a few months for me to get settled." Soon after, he inquired about signing me to the label, but everything had to be approved from the West Coast, and he was denied permission to sign any new artists. Later, he left Capitol and went over to United Artists and eventually produced Kenny Rogers's album *The Gambler* and . . . the rest is history.

Well, Larry told me to just have faith once again and wait a little while for him to make a plan for me. Of course, drug addicts have no patience, let alone political correctness or manners. I kept saying to myself, "This is it! I'm gonna hang a gold album on the wall, and then I'll tell everybody to go fuck off, just like I always said I would!"

After making it, my plan was to drive back to my hometown in a big Cadillac and give everybody I used to know the finger. As you can see, I was motivated from a purely creative, wholesome place. The truth is that at the time, I didn't have a genuine awareness of why I was so pissed off or even specifically *who* I was pissed off at. I was just pissed off.

By now, my amphetamine-and-alcohol habit was driving me further into an unconscious life. I called Larry once or twice a week, who pleaded with me, "Wyatt, I'm settling in here. Just give me time."

I couldn't. I wanted it so badly. I harassed him to the point where he refused to take my calls, and I haven't spoken to him in 30 years. If I hadn't been crazy, maybe I would have cut some hit records, but I probably would have died in the process. Who knows what would have happened?

I'm neither grateful nor sad that it didn't happen. It was all just part of the plan.

ↂ ↂ ↂ

Back at home, I was putting up a pretty good front. In fact, my booking agent had no idea that he was representing an addict. He didn't know that I had a problem because, to be perfectly honest, I'd never been in his office without about six drinks and a few pills in me. Years later, he'd say, "I never could tell you were high because I never saw you sober." This is an old adage I heard many times.

My agent also didn't see the times that I almost overdosed. One night, for example, I was at a club and went backstage and took about 700 milligrams of speed. It didn't seem like a big deal because I started using in 1961 with 15 milligrams a day, and now it was 11 years later. I needed more and more of the drug in my system in order to reach the hoped-for destination.

That night, I went to my dressing room, got high, and subsequently dropped into an almost coma-like sleep on the tattered couch. My guitar player found me, ran over, and rammed his finger down my throat. This caused me to throw up, and saved my life. Thank you, Johnny Walker (that was the guitar player's name). He has since passed away, as have several of the men who worked with me in those years. I was barely alive myself in those days. I walked around in what today would be called an amphetamine-induced psychosis. In other words, I was crazy.

I'd watch *Casper the Friendly Ghost,* a kiddie cartoon on TV, and break into tears because I felt so sorry for him. That's not exactly normal behavior. But let's face it, my nerves had been shattered. If someone made a sudden noise, I'd feel as if I were leaving my body. It would hit my system like a bomb. And to this day, I still have a bit of what's known as an "exaggerated startle response." It's getting better because of the therapeutic work I've done, but there are some souvenirs from the past that will never quite get put away.

But let's not get too far ahead of ourselves here. In my drug-addicted, alcoholic state, I wasn't exactly a model father to my boy. I consoled myself like most addicts do: by making excuses. Certainly, I wasn't harming my son, mostly because I wasn't home that much. But years later during therapy, Jarrod told me, "Dad, your leaving devastated me. I was terrified, because every time you'd leave, I wondered if you were going to die or never come back. All I wanted was a normal dad."

One Saturday night in November of 1975, I knew I was in serious trouble. I was standing onstage in Rochester, Minnesota, and I was in such a drug-induced nightmare that I was convinced that everyone in that audience was staring into the very depths of my soul. It was worse than being out there buck naked—it was like I was on display with my skin on inside out.

Out there in front of that audience, I was literally losing my mind, but I figured that it was best to do such a thing all by myself. So I threw down my microphone and ran off the stage. I ran out of the club and out of that city—I just kept running and running. And at that moment, I quit using amphetamines and went home to Nashville.

Days of darkness went by where I barely lifted the shade in my bedroom. I did get up long enough to pour all my pills down the toilet and flush them away. Coincidentally, in my suitcase was a half quart of whiskey. My mind told me to drink it until the last drop was gone. But something within made me uncap that bottle and pour it down the toilet, too. This wasn't an easy act for a man used to drinking close to two quarts of booze a day. But guess what? I was finally being a tough guy.

I went into massive withdrawal, and no amount of toughness can make that process easier. I just had to ride it out. I was pouring sweat and violently shaking. On top of what was happening to my body, I was also having severe hallucinations. I heard voices coming out of the air conditioner, and demonic visions were coming out of the curtains. Inside my head was a roar of pure terror. In the few lucid moments I had, I wished that I would die.

It was at this juncture, however, that through the grace of God, I was willing to see a doctor whom I still love to this day. He's one of the people who saved me from ending up as "the late Wyatt Webb."

❦ ❦ ❦   ❦ ❦ ❦

Chapter 4

ᏫᎡᏫᎡᏫ

The Gig Is Up

The doctor's name was Jack Kinnard. And the first thing he did was take my blood pressure, which was off the charts, especially for someone who was only 32 years old.

"My God, it's a wonder you're still alive," he said in a kindly voice. He didn't judge me; he only wanted to help me. And so, he was the first person in a long time who got something rare from me: the truth.

I told him how severe my habit had been—about 700 milligrams of speed and two quarts of liquor a day—but I could barely make eye contact with him because I felt so ashamed.

Dr. Kinnard didn't shake his head or wave a finger. He simply said, "Son, it's a miracle that you're able to breathe."

He performed a full physical on me and rushed the results. Two hours later, as he held the paperwork, his eyes were wide and confused. "This is the most incredible thing I've ever seen in my whole professional life," he finally said. "You shouldn't have a memory. You shouldn't even have a pulse. But you're actually healthy physically, except for this withdrawal, which will level out."

Ten drug-free days later, I went back to see Dr. Kinnard, and all my vital signs were normal. "Wyatt, you've really been handed a gift here," he said, rather bluntly. "Now what are you going to do with it?"

Dr. Kinnard mentioned a place that he knew of in Nashville called Cumberland Heights. This was a treatment facility where people with my problems went to heal, and it had been around since 1966.

Into my palm, Dr. Kinnard pressed a tiny white card with a woman's name—Carlene Hunt—on it. He said, "This is a woman I suggest you talk to, because she will understand."

"Thanks," I said, full of false bravado, "but I don't need to talk to anyone. I can do this myself."

Even though she would eventually change my entire life, I didn't meet Carlene for years. Why? Well, *I* didn't have a problem. There, in Dr. Kinnard's office, I actually had the nerve to think to myself, *I'm off drugs, but now I'm going to have to learn how to drink all over again.* At the time, I still didn't think I had a problem with alcohol.

Two years later, I still wasn't doing any drugs.

In fact, I'd been totally clean in that department since that day in the doc's office. But my old friend/nemesis alcohol was still calling. I actually made it for six weeks at one point without a drink—then I got a call to go back out on the road and sing. *I just won't drink anymore,* I thought to myself. *After all, I quit pills.*

But this was not to be the case: It took me two more years, until August 3, 1979, to stop drinking. That day, I sat in my home and informed my wife that I had a major problem with alcohol—it no longer gave me relief. She called Cumberland Heights, and I was admitted into treatment for addiction that very day. They told my wife, "Bring him out here right now before he changes his mind," and so she threw stuff in a suitcase as fast as her hands could carry it.

I met Carlene Hunt that night. Again, there were no judgment calls, and Dr. Kinnard was right: For the first time in my life, I felt like someone understood. Carlene told me about her history. You can imagine the relief I felt when she said these simple words: "As you can see, Wyatt, your life sounds a lot like my own. The only difference is that I'm on the other side of where you are now."

I desperately wanted to go where she was.

The third day I was at Cumberland Heights, I realized that I'd finally found a place where I could fit in. I didn't feel like an alien anymore. I felt it the minute I walked into a group therapy session. See, they got me out of the solo stuff like detox really fast because I was getting antsy and I wanted to run. After two days of that stuff, some men came to get me and took me to this cabin where people were just sitting around talking about their lives. Normally, I would have bolted from this sort of situation. But a middle-aged man came up to me and started talking about what he was going through in his life. All he wanted me to do was listen.

After a long time, one man said, "Now, how are you feeling?"

Feeling? I was the boy from Georgia who wasn't supposed to think about that f-word. Feeling? With swollen eyes, I told him how I was feeling, and he said nothing. All *I* wanted *him* to do was listen. And by the end of those few hours, I knew one thing for certain: I had finally found a family that was a perfect fit for me. How did I know this? Well, in the middle of talking about myself, something terrible happened: I felt my stomach go into hyperwhirl, and I knew that I was about to throw up.

"Excuse me!" I cried, jumping up and running outside to the bushes. Two men ran out with me—one of them held me around my stomach, the other ran inside and got a wet cloth.

"Go for it, Big Guy," the first one said. "You should've seen *me* a couple of weeks ago."

The second man emerged from the cabin with a

washcloth and wiped my face down.

I was overwhelmed and humbled by the kindness of these absolute strangers. At first, my eyes shimmered with tears, and the next thing we knew, three grown men were standing over some gross gunk and laughing our asses off. We had all been there before.

That night, they picked me up from detox to take me to the inpatient 12-step meeting, where 33 abused bodies sat in a tiny, smoke-filled room. Each night, somebody got up and told their story. Well, I was sitting in the back that first night, shaking at the very prospect, when this guy announced, "Everybody, there's a new guy sitting way in the back. Why don't you come up here, Big Guy, and tell us your story."

"Holy Jesus," I muttered. Then again, I had been onstage many times in my life. My brain said, "You're not chickenshit." My body, however, said something else. Trembling legs barely carried me to the front of the room and nearly buckled when I looked into these faces of compassion. The first thing I said was, "Can I sit down?"

"Of course," they said in unison, like it was the chorus of a beautiful song.

And I told them my entire life story. I told them about being an alien and an addict. I talked about the pills, the pressure, and the peace that was so lacking in my life. I talked about things so heavy that as I released each ugly word, it was as if the bulldozer that had been resting on my chest for most of my life finally kicked into gear and moved a few inches away. As my story went on, the bulldozer inched farther and farther off my breast plate until it was parked somewhere else. Somewhere far away.

I took the first deep breath I'd had in years. There was a lightness to me that left me practically giddy. And afterwards, one by one, my new family came up and hugged me. "God, I wouldn't have had the courage to tell that story so soon," said one middle-aged man.

In that moment, I finally figured out what *courage* really meant in this life.

I was the kid who always thought I was chicken-shit, and I had been terrified for most of my life. In treatment, people were suddenly loving me for *me*. Unconditionally. I had told them the goriest, most horrible stuff about myself . . . and they hugged me for it. This was what I had been looking for forever—a place to fit in.

After ten days of being in treatment, I heard someone else describe *courage*. They said, "Courage is being afraid and going ahead and trying anyway."

I always thought courage had to do with being fearless. But when I heard that you could be afraid and still be courageous, a light went on in my head. I said, "I'm probably one of the most courageous people on this planet because I've been terrified my whole life, and I'm still here."

Maybe in some people's eyes, my life wasn't good enough or it seemed like I had copped out. But they didn't know—they hadn't lived in this skin. This body and soul had gone through what author Joseph Campbell called "the hero's journey." Here, Campbell talks about the purification of going into "the abyss" and "slaying the dragon." It certainly felt as if I had slain one hell of a dragon. To boil Campbell's theory down, he essentially said that self-awareness is the gift you're rewarded with if you make it through the abyss and come out on the other side. Well, I made it though the darkest times and came out the other side. And yeah, I finally had a little bit of awareness and acceptance of myself. And no matter what anybody else said, that was good enough for me.

⤫   ⤫   ⤫

I've certainly shaken hands with the devil, if one exists. And now, I've saved the story I'm about to tell you for this moment because it's the most horrible one I've got.

Many months prior to my going into treatment, I sat alone on the side of my bed with a rifle barrel in my mouth. I was in so much pain that I couldn't figure out what else to do. But I couldn't pull the trigger. As that cold metal taste trickled across my tongue, I fingered the trigger, but old chickenshit couldn't go through with it.

The truth was, I wasn't chickenshit. I'd simply chosen to try again.

Years later, when I would work with those who were suicidal, I would tell them that story. I'd say, "If I hadn't had the option of suicide on more than one occasion, I probably would have killed myself." There was something strangely life-affirming about knowing I could do it yet decide not to.

Choosing to get clean and sober was also life-affirming. As I went through the program, I discovered that I had the emotional maturity of an 11-year-old boy. Basically, I didn't have a clue how to cope with life. All I knew was how to survive, which is a whole other animal. And despite the fact that I did everything they told me to do in treatment, I was still scared.

I later learned that there was a little wager going through the treatment population at Cumberland Heights. The bet was that there were two of us who wouldn't make it. One guy was in the music–publishing business. The other was me.

We both stayed sober.

I wish that I could write "happy ending" at this point, but actually, this was more like a "happy beginning."

In treatment, one of the staff's suggestions was that I quit the music business, for they feared that the environment would cause me to relapse. Well, that just wasn't a realistic option at the time. I knew no other way of earning a living, and I had bills to pay. And so, four weeks out of treatment, my agent booked me for a week-long engagement in Sault Ste. Marie, Ontario, Canada.

My sponsor, Harold, and another guy in the support group (whom I lovingly referred to as "Grumpy") privately got together and told each other, "That SOB won't make it three days."

They were my supporters! But they said, "Too much temptation. He shouldn't be working clubs."

I didn't know about this until much later. What I *did* know, in the deepest place I knew of so far, was that I *would* make it. I knew when I left treatment that I would be a man of my word and never drink again as long as I lived. In the recovery community, that sounded dangerous, I know. But I had become willing to do whatever was necessary to stay clean. I knew that drugs and alcohol were simply no longer a part of my deal. I truly had gone through a process of spiritual surrender.

One year later, I was still totally sober. And on the anniversary of my first year of sobriety, my sponsor and Grumpy sat in the front row of our group meeting dressed in suits and ties in my honor. That night, they told the story of how they feared for me before that Ontario job some 12 months before. How were they to know that I had faith in, and a relationship with, a newfound God? I had also become willing to do something different, which was to follow the directions given to me by the recovering community that I'd adopted as my family of choice.

I was waking up, for I'd been asleep far too long.

Chapter 5

Spiritual Surrender

It may appear that I've skipped over a large portion of my journey thus far. I've even used the phrase "spiritual surrender" without much explanation. I've saved that for now because it's one of the most meaningful segments of this story.

As you may already have guessed, I spent many years of my life angry with the God of my childhood religion. Maybe my entire life was spent treating God as the enemy. After all, I was the kid who was forced to attend a church that told me I was damned from the start. For that reason, I never really had any sort of intimate relationship with a higher power.

I did believe in the *existence* of God. I felt that someone had to have jump-started the entire solar system into existence—it seemed that there was just too much order for this to be some quirk or cosmic happenstance. But I just didn't see *myself* connected to

God in any which way. The closest things I found resembling God were drugs and alcohol. They lifted my spirits—at least for a little while. When those substances were gone, however, I was left with nothing.

I had been in treatment for about a week, and the director of therapy, a woman by the name of Bunny Blankman, had been away on vacation. I kept hearing her name, though, and one day she appeared, telling me that my presence was required at a lecture she was giving to the entire patient population. So I ambled into the meeting room and sat in my usual place—way in the back with my arm hanging out the only window.

There was a back-door entrance into this main lecture room, and suddenly it opened and Bunny walked in. It was as if the room had just become brighter. She was a striking woman who simply smiled and said good morning. But her eyes! It was as if there were sparks flying out of them. I felt her looking right at me as she told her story.

Bunny's demons had been sedatives and alcohol. She shared with us a life of devastation similar to mine. She then talked about going to her first recovery meeting, and it was heartbreaking.

She told us that she saw the word *God* on the wall and started to cry.

A man seated next to her asked, "Bunny, what's wrong?"

"This won't work for me because I'm an atheist!"

The man gazed warmly at her and said, "That's all right. It *will* work for you if you can just believe in a power greater than yourself. Can you start by just believing in *us* as that power?"

"Y-yes," she stammered.

That gave her hope when there was none. It turns out that Bunny *could* believe in a higher power. An atheist had come to believe in God! That said everything to me. If a former atheist could have a personal relationship with God, then so could I. Looking into Bunny's eyes, I knew one thing for sure: I wanted to experience what she was feeling in her heart that made her sparkle so. I wanted to feel that kind of happiness.

That was a huge moment in my life.

I walked up to Bunny after her lecture and said, "I want to thank you for introducing me to a God it may be possible for me to hang out with, because the One I was raised with is Someone I don't really want to know."

She looked at me with a knowing, soft sense of understanding.

That's where it began for God and me.

Finding God didn't necessarily mean that I was looking at sunshine and roses and halos, even though there *were* times when I heard the angels sing and felt the sweetness of divine grace. Primarily what it meant was that I was going to be given opportunities to grow, but this would also require some hard work.

Another heavy hitter was about to join the lineup of this team of truth merchants. His name was Logan Morrell. He was in his late 50s, with thinning hair, a big nose, and a wonderfully warm smile. He had retired from NASA when he was called into service at Cumberland Heights by the executive director.

Quite simply, Logan was the man who was largely responsible for silencing the voices that were screaming in my head. This wasn't an easy job, because ever since I was a kid, I'd been besieged by several committees in my mind who knew how to do nothing but criticize.

I didn't know what to do about these voices. I was afraid I wouldn't survive them, but I was more afraid that I was destined to live with them. The professionals dubbed what I was experiencing as "auditory hallucinations." Well, no matter what you called it, one of those voices I kept hearing was always cursing God. It would just come out of nowhere, and I wondered if my hellfire-and-brimstone upbringing had anything to do with it. Who knows? Who cares? Something just needed to be done about it.

When I would think and hear the most horrible things related to God early on, I would look up in the sky, expecting to get popped by lightning. It never happened. But I knew there was something terribly wrong with my head. My heart didn't have anything against the Deity. I thought to myself, *What is this about?*

I worried that I'd been possessed by evil spirits.

Somewhere around this time, *The Exorcist* was released into movie theaters. The fact that I went to see that movie, as fragile as my psyche was at the time, is probably evidence of my insanity.

Anyway, I finally couldn't take it anymore, so I requested some time with Logan. One of his best qualifications for being an alcoholism counselor was that he had been sober for a number of years, so he had some awareness of the terrain.

Logan was sarcastic and quick-witted. He said very little and rarely minced words. I liked him. But I also instantly trusted him.

In my entire life, I had never told anybody about the cursing-God thing. With only ten days between me and my last drink, I sat down with Logan to tell him about my secret problem.

"Well, here's what I'm going to suggest that you do," Logan responded. "Every day when you walk that half mile to the gate [which is what we did for exercise on most days], I want you to practice what I call 'prayer and meditation.'"

My face went blank.

"What do you know about prayer and meditation?" he queried.

"Well . . . ," I began.

"Nah, I know that you don't know anything," he said, adding, "prayer is talking, and meditation is listening. Period. So on your walk to the gate, I want you to talk to God or whoever you think is going to take this away from you. And when the cursing voice starts to come to you, I want you to raise your right hand and say, 'I command you to leave my thought process, in the name of Almighty God Himself.'"

All I could think at the time was, *Oh my God, he's nuts. This is all the shit I hate.* He sounded like some damn evangelist.

"Isn't there another way to do this?" I begged.

"Yeah," said Logan, "you can keep doing it your way, Wyatt. And we both know how well that's served you. You need to stop wasting my damn time if you're not willing to do what I suggest!"

He paused, peering intently at me. I agreed to follow his suggestion.

"Okay," he said, narrowing his eyes. "Then I want you to walk all the way to the gate and raise your hand to stop the voice as many times as you need. On the way back from the gate, shut your mouth and just listen."

I left his office thinking that the old bastard was as crazy as a loon. But the one thing that stuck with me was that as I was walking out, he stopped me and asked, "What do you have to lose?"

Honestly, I didn't have an answer to that question.

The next day, I walked to the gate, and here came the voice. It said, "Goddamn God!" My head bobbed around to see if anybody was looking, but there was nobody around. So I raised my right hand, repeated what Logan had told me to say, and then jerked my hand down as fast as I could. I could feel the blood rushing to my ears in embarrassment.

On the way back from the gate, I listened, but the voice kept talking to me. I went straight to Logan's office and said, "I did exactly what you said, and it didn't work!"

Logan looked up from his paperwork and said, "Did I give you a time limit? You keep doing what I said. And don't keep coming back in here tomorrow and the next day telling me it didn't work. *I'll* let you know when I need to know something from you."

Four days later, I woke up and suddenly realized that the night before when I'd said a prayer, I heard . . . nothing. The silence was pure bliss. I waited and heard . . . not a peep. That morning, the voice didn't speak. And it hasn't spoken since.

As you might imagine, I couldn't wait to see Logan. I threw on some clothes early that morning and went running to his office. He hadn't arrived yet. I waited anxiously to tell him because I knew it was over. When he arrived, I rushed toward him, exclaiming, "Logan, I've got to see you!"

"Would you let me get a damn cup of coffee?" he muttered.

I got his coffee for him, and then we went back to his office where I told him what had happened. With tears in his eyes, he reached across the desk and touched my hand. I started crying when I said, "You'll never know how much I appreciate what you told me to do. How did you know this was going to work?"

He smiled and admitted, "Wyatt, I had no idea it was going to work."

"Surely you've tried this with other people," I said.

To which he replied, "I've never told anybody to do such a damn stupid thing in my life."

"You tricked me!" I cried.

"How does it feel?" he retorted. "You've been doing shit like this to people for about 20 years!"

I admitted that, at that moment, it felt pretty fucking good.

"I want to tell you something," Logan said. "You're about as hungry as anybody I've ever seen come through here. You're hungry for peace of mind. I suspect there have been times when you've almost lost your mind."

"That's true," I said, choking up.

And then, Logan said something that changed my entire life, which certainly bears repeating: "Whether or not you get what you're looking for depends on one thing and one thing only," he said. "It depends on your willingness to do something different."

I was 36 years old when I left his office that day, but I was just becoming a man. And I've been sharing that one sentence with people ever since Logan Morrell's words became part of my knowledge base some 22 years ago.

I was amazed by what opened up to me from that moment forward. I suspected that my days in the music business were numbered, although I stayed on the road awhile longer. I continued to work three more years on the road after rehab, despite the fact that everyone wondered if it would be too hard for me to work in clubs.

It wasn't difficult from a sobriety standpoint. I'll admit it was painfully boring, but I never had the desire to drink again because of two things. First, I was doing something different; and second, there was always somebody in those clubs behaving the way I used to. A drunk would walk up in my face, slurring his words and acting absurd. I'd say, "This poor bastard is going to wake up in the morning, and I know just how he's going to feel—it's going to be awful."

I would look at these former cohorts and think to myself, *God, I don't have to do that anymore. I'm going to go to bed tonight and wake up tomorrow without my skin crawling. I won't have to throw up. I'm not going to be paranoid. I'm not going to wonder what I did last night—and how bad I did it or how well.*

At first, I worried about my ability to perform. How would I still be funny onstage without the booze? Then I thought, *Shit, Wyatt. You haven't been funny for quite some time now.*

It took about six months for me to feel as natural as I was going to feel onstage. And two and a half years later, I made the decision to quit being an entertainer for good. I remember performing in Colorado one night, thinking, *All I'm doing is playing background music so somebody can get laid tonight. This is it. This is my life's work. And this isn't fun anymore. It's no longer important to me.*

Remember when you were back in school and thought you wanted to be a teacher? Then you went to the hospital one day and thought you wanted to be a doctor? Your house was on fire, and you thought, *I can work the extinguisher, so maybe I could be a fire-fighter.* Well, a lot of people in rehab think, *I know, I'll become a counselor.* That crossed my mind. By the way, have I mentioned that my college degree was in English with a minor in psychology?

As for the English part, I can't talk without swearing. And psychology? Well, I've been nuts most of my life. But both of these "skills" would come in pretty handy later on.

ை௫ை ௫ை ௫ை ௫ை ௫ை ௫ை

Chapter 6

ᑫᑫᑫᑫ

Treating the
Wounded Spirit

It's funny how life changes for the better in what
seem to be the strangest ways. After I got off the
road and quit my singing career, my life did a complete
180. Unfortunately, as is sometimes the case, my marriage did not survive sobriety. Four years after I got
out of rehab, my wife and I got a very amicable
divorce. (And in 1995, I would meet Carin, the angel
who ended up becoming my second wife. More on her
later.) My son, Jarrod, who was 17 when his mom and
I split up, went on to college and his own life. And as
for me, I was offered a job at the place where I got
sober.

I'd stayed in touch with sparkling-eyed Bunny, and
I occasionally mentioned to her that someday I might
want some work. When that someday came, she was
glad to bring me in, figuring that I had about a lifetime

of experience in what's known as "living a hard life." My education also became valuable at that time. I hadn't known up until then why I'd even bothered to get a college degree—other than that it beat the hell out of going to work.

Over the course of the next 20 years, I would add a wide range of therapeutic modalities to my academic training. These included studying altered states of consciousness (without the handicap of drugs), Gestalt therapy, psychodrama, family systems, cross-cultural communications, and holotrophic breath work (a therapeutic tool that combines deep, continuous breathing with evocative music designed to tap in to each energy chakra in the body). Most recently, holographic memory resolution work was added to my résumé thanks to its creator, Dr. Brent Baum. (In Chapter 17, I'll tell you more about this remarkable man.)

I seemed to have a natural gift for therapy, but of course I had to learn how to listen in the most conscious and reverent of ways. Bunny helped by putting me through the works, teaching me how to develop treatment plans, and how to document progress or lack of it. Then she gave me a group and reminded me that sharing my own story was part of the deal.

My first patient was a guy named Jackie. He was this very sweet man from Gallatin, Tennessee. He was also your basic alcoholic. Yet from what I've heard, he's still sober today. I was hungry to help this man because I really wanted to give something back in light of how my life was handed back to *me*. Soon, people with addictions became my specialty, and I met all sorts of wonderful characters from all walks of life. I assisted addicts of all kinds—even people in the music business—from 1979 to 1992.

Before I knew it, I was working with kids in Nashville. A short time later, after what amounted to a phone interview, I was hired by the Sierra Tucson treatment facility in Arizona to set up an adolescent-care program.

And so, I came out to the desert. It wasn't my first time in this very spiritual, energized, mystical part of the country. I'd first visited Arizona several years previously, on my way to California. I said to myself, "Someday, I'm gonna live in Tucson." I wish I could tell you that this was for some deep, profound reason, but the truth is, it was all about those John Wayne Westerns that were filmed in Old Tucson. Man, I loved those movies when I was a kid, and I'd seen that landscape so many times. So, when I drove through this area on my trip to California, I was finally able to see it in person, and the only thought going through my mind was, *God, I just want to be here.*

I settled in to my job at Sierra Tucson, and I began to do group work. Shortly afterwards, they moved me to a management position. I eventually became the program director of the facility. It finally felt like the major leagues, as Sierra Tucson is one of the premier treatment centers in the world. Some time went by, and I was offered the job of executive director of the adult facility, which really humbled me. My God, that they would trust me with that job! It was a dream come true, and I was offered more money than I'd ever made in my entire life. But the paycheck was only one part of it for me. And after a brief tenure in this position, I was given executive directorship of the newly constructed Sierra Tucson Adolescent Care Facility.

In that mountain hideaway, we were doing exciting stuff, and I loved the unconventional therapies we were allowed to engage in—one of which involved horses.

ॐ   ॐ   ॐ

Let me stop for a moment and tell you about horses and me. I'd been fascinated with unicorns since I was a kid. The unicorn was supposedly a mythical animal that spent its entire life trying to regain its gentle nature. I felt that they were a lot like I was, and I pretty much established the unicorn as a spiritual symbol for myself. But as for flesh-and-blood equines, you might think that in Georgia, I would have had experience with horses galore. Sure, I wanted one as a kid, and I always admired them—but I never got a chance to call one my own. Yet every single time I'd get the chance, I'd stop along the road to gaze at the horses that lived at a nearby farm.

I would watch them run with such grace that it actually brought tears to my eyes. I don't know what I found so captivating about them, other than that I was simply drawn to their spirit. To look at a galloping horse would just inspire me (and it still does). It was about freedom and power and beauty. If God could have had a physical manifestation on Earth, I thought He would have been a horse.

When a horse has both nostrils flaring and his eyes are ablaze, it's the damnedest thing I've ever seen. It's pure joy, and an incredible force. The secret is that horses aren't just joyful for a few precious moments in their day like most humans are—they're that way *all* the time.

Sadly, my first experience on a horse was not transforming. An entertainer friend of mine in Nashville invited me to his house. I was drunk, but we decided to go riding anyway (something I absolutely do not recommend). The horse walked under a tree, simply because I didn't know how to steer him away from it—it's also entirely possible that I was too messed up to even see that tree. Well, that trip under the mighty oak introduced me to a low-hanging limb that knocked me off the horse, and in the process, broke my nose. It's a wonder I didn't get killed.

Of course, I blamed the horse. I said, "I don't want anything else to do with this dumb-ass thing." But *I* was the dumb ass of the situation. That poor horse had to deal with a crazy drunk on his back.

At the time, it was appropriate that I said, "It's the horse's fault." It was a running theme for me that I'd make up stories about others, and I wasn't taking responsibility for my life at all. The good news is that, years later, I would get to teach this lesson from my own experience. My habit of making up stories about others was nothing more than my talking about myself. I just wasn't able to see that at the time.

Years later, as a sober person, I looked at horses, saw their power, and found myself in awe once again. Their therapeutic powers just make sense. In fact, for many years, horses have been used as therapists for children with neuromuscular disease, Down's syndrome, and a myriad of other challenging disorders. It's called "hippo therapy" (*hippo* is the Latin word for "horse"). My understanding of hippo therapy is that the natural movement of a horse will realign the body of a human being. In other words, horses were the world's original chiropractors.

For example, let's say you're having back trouble. If you can get on a horse (unless you have disc problems), the animal can assist in realigning the skeletal system. I can vouch for this, because I once suffered from sciatica. It was so severe that I couldn't even move at times.

But I started to ride horses, and I haven't had this problem since. Just keep in mind that for best results, you have to make sure *you don't resist the movement of the horse.*

The body and the spirit are all part of the same energy system. In fact, I heard famed writer and therapist Jacquelyn Small proclaim years ago that we're not human beings having a spiritual experience, we're spiritual beings having a human experience. This defied everything I was told as a child . . . and made perfect sense. So why not treat one's wounded spirit with a horse?

෴   ෴   ෴

Let's get back to Sierra Tucson. When I took the job as executive director, there was a program in place involving humans and horses interacting with each other. However, I had a problem with this program almost immediately because too often I had seen people anthropomorphize animals (basically assigning them human traits), and I was afraid that this was what was happening. For example, I'd hear, "The horse appears to be depressed today and is acting out." I even heard a staff member begin to assign dysfunctional family roles to the herd. One horse was the "scapegoat," another was the "hero." Since I felt that this practice wasn't true or helpful,

I stopped it.

As I watched the program unfold, a lot of what I saw made sense in theory, but it wasn't being manifested clearly in practice. I took my time watching and waiting, and at the time, I resisted being my hair-trigger, opinionated self.

The truth was that I knew very little about horses, but I could clearly see what was possible when horses and humans came together. It was a defining moment in my life. I determined, at that point in time, that the program would become people-focused. I'd been trained over the course of ten years to know that all behavior is learned, and the good news was that just because something had been learned a certain way didn't mean that it had to be a life sentence. Not only was change possible, but if happiness was to be achieved, it was often necessary.

I explained to these kids that everything they knew regarding how to treat other living things was primarily learned from people. Bottom line: I knew that they'd treat the *horses* just like they'd been conditioned and taught to treat *people*. Behaviorally, the kids in the program had the opportunity, through their interaction with the horses, to look at what they'd learned: Was their behavior working for or against them? That they were in treatment at all was a testimony to the fact that they'd been grossly misinformed about what would work for them.

It was a simple fact that these kids had created dangerous situations in their lives prior to treatment, and each day at the stables, they were re-creating their lives before our very eyes. If the child was in conflict with a parent or peer, chances are that they'd create conflict with the horse. This had to be monitored closely, as it truly could become hazardous.

For example, one day a 16-year-old boy named Tommy was putting a saddle on a horse and was about to tighten the girth that holds it in place. He shoved his knee hard into the horse's abdomen in an effort to make the animal "relax." The horse was terrified and was on the verge of rearing up. If a staff member hadn't been there, it could have gotten really ugly. Later on, I found that Tommy's *life* was pretty ugly: He was the product of a home with an extremely dominant father who had modeled this type of behavior for the boy.

That day in the barn, Tommy and I talked about his life prior to treatment. He'd had problems with alcohol and drugs and had had some run-ins with the law. By the end of our session, he had learned a new way to saddle a horse that didn't have the potential to kill him. He was surprised and pleased to learn that there was another way.

Those kids were certainly full of surprises. The one constant was the horse.

I knew that working with horses was an extremely

powerful way for people to heal. In a nutshell, I clearly saw these animals as mirrors of people's internal selves. All people had to do was just interact with them, and the horses would respond or not respond in ways that would give us the opportunity to work with the person emotionally—if they were willing to go there.

I came to discover that the horses would always cooperate with whatever the humans asked them to do if, and only if, the human could and would give clear energetic direction to the horse. We're talking about simple body language, which is nothing more than a product of our energy system.

The energy system is going to operate either consciously or unconsciously—it's really up to us. A human being's energy system begins with a thought, and with each one, a little flame of energy is lit. An emotional response immediately accompanies each thought, which in turn fuels and magnifies the energy. What happens next is where energy turns into language. And there are literally thousands of expressions of the energy system.

As a result of what we think and feel, our bodies will automatically do one of three things: They'll either stay where they are, move forward, or back up. This happens automatically. So, wouldn't it behoove us to pay attention to what we're thinking and feeling, since the body will act it out anyway?

If we're not paying attention to what we think and

feel as it determines our behavior, it becomes impossible for us to give clear, energetic direction to the horse—or anybody else. If we *are* paying attention to what we're thinking or feeling, our communication is generally direct in nature and offers the being or person that we're in a relationship with the opportunity to respond in one of two ways: yes or no.

What this actually means is that the chances of getting our needs met are at least 50-50. In order to achieve this aim, we have to eliminate what we've been trained to do, which is to give mixed messages. See, horses don't understand these types of messages, so they become the perfect energy barometer to gauge whether or not we humans are communicating clearly.

Remember: *All connection comes about at an energetic level.* We're often led to believe that we connect through words, but it's been my experience that we actually use words more often to *avoid* communicating with each other.

Allow me to ask you one question about the relationships you've had in your life. If the relationship became problematic and there was a block to communication, intimacy, or any kind of meaningful connection, was it usually emotionally based? More often than not, the answer to this question is yes. This is because of two feelings that are the universal enemies of humankind: fear and self-doubt.

We're not born with these two problems—they're

learned from the various systems we're exposed to during our stay on this planet. In varying degrees of severity, fear and self-doubt have been predominant in every client I've ever worked with my entire life. They appear to be the impediments to our evolution as a species and are the areas where many of us are individually stuck. Included here is the fear of being seen, the fear of not being enough, the fear of making a mistake, and the fear of getting emotionally or physically hurt.

The more I saw it happen, the more I realized that working with a horse can help to identify what's causing a person's particular fear or self-doubt; the horse can then help that person overcome their challenges. I thought to myself, *Here it is. This might possibly help solve some of the problems in our world.*

Yes, I'm a dreamer and grandiose at times, but you know something? To the core of my soul, I truly believe that the powerful combination of horse and human is an avenue to awareness.

I felt a deep need to communicate this revelation to the staff at Sierra Tucson—and to anyone else who would listen. I didn't have a manual, but I had first-hand experience. I knew that if people could be authentic and "become still" internally, then nature itself would draw closer to them.

How did I know this to be true? In the summer of 1985, I was attending a nine-day retreat in Minnesota. Every day was dedicated to growing spiritually through self-awareness. Some six days into the workshop, I'd taken a walk into the nearby woods. All of a sudden, walking up behind me was a very large brown feathered bird with white specks. I think it was a grouse of some kind; I also think it was female. At first, she frightened me—God only knows why. I guess it was because no wild creature had ever come that close to me in a nonthreatening way. Anyway, that bird followed me for some 200 yards, feeding on the insects that my steps were unearthing.

I found myself in a surreal place internally. I was in total awe of the sacredness of that particular moment. I only had one explanation at the time, which had to do with the deep emotional and spiritual work I was engaged in during the workshop: My energy had become so calm and peaceful that I posed absolutely no threat to the grouse. I guess she felt safe with me. I was more present with myself that day than I had ever been in my life. In other words, I had come home to a place of authenticity in my body.

I know now that that connection can *only* occur through authenticity. If I don't know who I am, or if I perceive that I need to withhold any part of who I am, then I've eliminated the possibility of connecting with *any* living thing. Authenticity, therefore, is the key to connection with horses. And it's the key to connection with humans, too.

∽ ∽ ∽

It's funny, but even though I was the director of this $8 million facility at Sierra Tucson, I had a lot of trouble staying focused on the computer screen and the stacks of paper on my desk. Each day as I sat in my beautiful, posh office, my eyes would gaze down longingly at the roof of that barn, and I'd find myself thinking, *I wonder what's going on down there today.*

I'd sit there and think about some of the kids I'd worked with, like Billy. Billy was one of our first clients, and he had a sizable alcohol and drug problem. He was an explosive teenager and dealt with his pain mostly with anger-based behaviors. Billy also had what appeared to be a mean streak—but in reality, it turned out to be a fear-and-pain streak.

Billy didn't know how *not* to be defensive, for he had no idea of how to deal with his fear. He simply wanted to be loved, but you'd never know this if you only looked at his external behavior. Little did he know that a beautiful young quarter horse named Lady was about to become one of his master teachers.

Early on, Lady had caught Billy's eye, but when he would approach her, the horse would avoid him. Again, at this point in time, I didn't know a damn thing about horses, but I had seen on more than one occasion a horse walk over to people when they were relaxed and experiencing an absence of fear. I immediately thought to myself, *All this kid has to do is acknowledge that he's hurting.*

One day at the barn, when he approached Lady and she walked away from him, Billy looked really pissed. I walked up to him cautiously and very simply said, "Are you scared or hurting, Billy? Or both?"

"Nobody gives a damn," he said.

I began to talk to him, and we started with his rage. I let him know that it was okay that he felt anger—it just wasn't okay for him to act it out. As minutes passed and I continued to listen to him, he began to acknowledge that he was afraid. Slowly, he became more comfortable talking about his fear; then he began to talk about his shame. Finally, he was able to express some of the pain and loneliness that had been passing for his life.

Lady had been standing some 80 feet away from Billy at the time. Suddenly, we heard hooves approaching. As we looked up, Lady had walked from where she was standing and was breathing on Billy's arm. Then she did something incredible: She began to nuzzle this child.

Billy didn't say anything, but he looked at me and looked back at the horse. He looked at me again and looked back at Lady. And then he began to cry for the first time in years.

After he left treatment, his mother called me and said that the work that Billy did with Lady that day helped give him his life back. She said that on that day, he had become a little boy again.

Prior to the incident with Billy, I had worked with

kids for three years. At that time, the therapeutic community had accepted that it generally took between two and three weeks to establish trust with a kid so that you could work with them. With the horses' help, it was regularly happening in the *first week*. Kids were getting well. In fact, I'm convinced that the horses were a major component of the success of many kids walking around right now who are drug free and doing positive things with their lives.

But just as everything seemed to be on the upswing, the bottom fell out. Sadly, it turned out that inpatient treatment for minors is extremely costly to provide—even more than adult treatment. Insurance companies suddenly stopped paying for children to go to inpatient treatment, which was insane. Here was an opportunity to intervene in some craziness that would save them billions of dollars later on. But unfortunately, no such foresight would prove to be in place.

When the insurance companies stopped paying, kids couldn't afford to come to treatment, and in 1993, the program came to an end. As a result, the facility was forced to let me go, and there were no other such jobs available in Tucson at that time. It was very hard to realize that a dream of mine seemed to be dying. Little did I know what lay in store for me.

At the time, however, my future looked bleak. This was an extremely depressing time for me. I went through grief over the loss of my program and the daily interaction with the kids. I immediately got caught up in self-doubt and fear. The first thing I thought was, *Oh my God, I'm going to lose my home. Will I ever get another job? What am I going to do?*

Of course, there was no evidence to support any of these sleep-robbing worries, but I had lost my job and I was scared—so I went right back to being eight years old. Soon, I was able to transcend that feeling when the facility awarded me a really generous severance package. For the first time in a long time, I was able to take some time and consider with a modicum of clarity what the next step needed to be in my life.

I was at another crossroads, only this time I was 47 years old. And just like when I was 18, I had to figure out what I wanted to do with the rest of my life.

∽ ∽ ∽ ∽ ∽ ∽

PART II

Waking Up
(a.k.a. "Reality")

Chapter 7

∾∾∾∾∾

It's Not about the Horse

Many years ago, I went through an extensive period where I was looking for my answers in the New Age world. I call this my "metaphysical-avoidance period" or "time spent at Woo-Woo U."

See, I had become fascinated with spiritual matters and was convinced that the answers I sought might possibly be found in the realm of metaphysics. Yet, no matter how much material I absorbed on this subject, I kept encountering one consistent message: *Each person has their own answer, which cannot be found externally.*

I finally exhausted the possibility of finding my answers in this area of study and was forced to go deeper into my own psyche and soul to find the answers to my questions. Believe it or not, this ended up being a rather painful time for me, for it was actually the re-creation of an addictive process—looking for relief externally.

It was during this time of transition that a colleague of mine said, "I have something you should listen to, Wyatt." He handed me a tape of a person who channels spirits from another world. You can only imagine my reaction to that one: *Oh my God, I thought I graduated from Woo-Woo U—and I'm certainly not interested in an advanced degree.*

One day, out of respect for my colleague (and some basic curiosity, too), I took the tape out of its case and halfheartedly pushed it into my stereo. Well, you could have knocked me over with a feather after what happened next. The channeler, speaking in a voice unlike any I'd ever heard, was conducting a question-and-answer period with the people in his workshop. A lady stepped up to the microphone and said, "I came to the workshop this weekend trying to determine the purpose of my being on the planet. What should I do with my life? Can you help with me that?"

And to my surprise, the next thing I heard has become part of my own personal mantra for success.

The channeler whispered, "Sure. What excites you the most? Next question."

I got it.

I said, "I'm going to take a year off and allow what excites me the most to surface." I already had an idea of what it was, but I was determined not to be impulsive.

Over the course of that year, I started training

with a Lithuanian dressage master by the name of Jonas Irbinskas. Although Jonas was in his late 60s and only 5'9", he was solidly built and quite a character. His accent was heavy, and I don't think he owned a clean pair of riding breeches. And he always wore a Swiss yodeler's cap, which was full of feathers people had given him or he'd found on the ground.

Jonas was an absolute joy to be around. Looking in his eyes was akin to looking at a wonder of nature. And though I'm sure he wasn't even aware of it, he became the only mentor I've ever chosen to have. Not a day passes that I don't remember something he told me.

As a matter of fact, he said something to me on my first day of training with him. He only said this phrase to me once, but it's stuck with me my whole life and has become my own little motto (in fact, it's the title of this book).

Jonas had assigned me a huge Irish thoroughbred to ride. After I had groomed and tacked up the horse, I mounted him and rode approximately 100 yards to the dressage arena where Jonas awaited. The horse was all over the place—his nostrils were flaring, and he was snorting and moving sideways, tossing his head wildly.

Let's just say I was quite frustrated.

When I rode into the middle of the arena, I looked over at Jonas and asked, "What did you feed this damn thing this morning?"

That's when he informed me as to the correct nature of things. He actually deigned to get out of his chair, walk to the middle of the arena, and take the horse by the reins. He then looked up at me and said, "First lesson from Jonas. Are you listening?"

I said, "Yes, sir."

He looked me square in the eye and said, "It's never the goddamn horse. It's not about the horse!"

Jonas then turned and started to walk back to his chair. But before he'd taken three steps, I had the nerve to ask, "Are you sure?"

He turned and shot back, "I knew you were going to say that. Get off the horse!"

Then he put his foot in the stirrup, mounted the horse, and that thoroughbred looked as if someone had tranquilized him. Jonas then put the horse through every possible move he could make athletically, and the horse actually looked *happy* while he was responding to his rider's every request.

At the conclusion of his demonstration, Jonas rode the horse up to where I was standing, dismounted, glared at me, and snapped, "Any more questions?"

"No sir," I said. And I meant it. I never questioned him again. I just did as I was told.

Jonas was always able to prove anything he said, and he's had an impact on my life in the same way that Logan Morrell did all those years ago. *When the student is ready, the master teacher truly does appear.*

Throughout my time with Jonas, I had become aware that I was communing with the horses spiritually. There was an ease in my relationship with them, which I could only attribute to the horses not seeing me as a threat.

I began to love the smell of horses and everything that surrounds these wonderful animals. All I could think about was horses and humans in relationships with each other and what that could mean.

Six months into the gift of my imposed vacation, I said, "*This* is definitely what excites me the most." And in a moment of pure clarity, I decided that I would make it my life's work. For those who said I didn't have a leg to stand on, well, hell, if I had me, one client, and a horse, then we had eight legs to stand on.

I absolutely refused to give in to self-doubt and fear this time. There have been points in my life when I've just had to declare: "This is what I plan to do." I was fortunate that I'd been taught over the years how to make my dreams come true. I truly believe that the universe will totally support what you're doing if you're willing to take some inspiration and mix it with perspiration.

The next step resulted in my going to see just about every therapist I knew to tell them about the new "horse-therapy" I was developing. I gave them a card announcing my new "office," which was a tan six-stall barn, the owner of which had said that she didn't care what I did in there.

So I went out and bought a horse. I paid $2,500 for this little bay-colored Arab named Dreamer. He was a beautiful horse whose name fit the general atmosphere of the time.

I knew *I* was a dreamer, but I was a dreamer who was willing to work. Sure, I had no clients, but I put the word out around Tucson, and then I waited. Eight weeks later, I had a case load of six people. Word of mouth went into motion, and the next thing I knew, I was busy.

During this time, I had also started to do consulting work for the facility that had been forced to let me go. Corporations were hiring me to do team-building work and to help them identify blocks in their system. What's interesting is that every one of the organizations I worked with basically suffered from one problem: faulty communication.

And guess what? Those communication problems were rooted in self-doubt and fear.

My own particular fear of not having enough work and becoming homeless had become a moot point. I bought two more horses, and I was making a good living. I didn't have all that administrative work to do. I was a happy man.

My work was based on what Logan had told me that day in his office so many years ago: If you have the desire for some peace of mind and feel the need to grow, you need to do one thing and one thing only—"something different."

I've probably looked people in the eye thousands of times over the last few years and said, "What do you have to lose by doing something different?" Doing something different is an opportunity available to each of us at every moment of our lives. And I base much of my work on this statement because of what it did for my own soul.

✍ ✍ ✍

Speaking of doing something different, one day the NextHealth Corporation approached me about joining a project known as "Miraval," which was to be a world-class resort they were in the process of building in Tucson. The match had been lit, and the fire was about to start. I told the NextHealth people how I wanted to work, along with what I was willing to do. They asked me to write a proposal outlining a program that would offer my work to their guests on a daily basis.

As I've previously mentioned, I'd been taught how to manifest things, so I was able to manifest the practice I have today by determining what excited me the most and combining that with the resources available to me.

When I presented my program to NextHealth, I found that they were in complete agreement with what I wanted to do, so it was easy for them to say, "This looks like a no-brainer. Bring your horses and let's do it." Their response was extremely encouraging to me. I'm continually filled with gratitude for the opportunity of doing what I love as a means of earning my living. And there has been a huge amount of support offered to me by countless numbers of gifted and generous people.

I was asked to write a mission statement. The one I wrote was to offer the premier program at the resort. Understand, there are many wonderful programs at Miraval, but from its inception, the Equine Experience has been referred to as the "signature program" of our facility.

So it began. Horses and humans. From the start on the Miraval grounds, the program was magic. Clients found that the Equine Experience was unlike anything they'd ever done in their lives.

Now, I'm not pointing any fingers at other programs that help internally. Yoga is a wonderful thing. Meditation is a wonderful thing. Everything we do here at Miraval is wonderful. But I don't think I've ever seen anything as wonderful as a horse and a human hooking up, and the human allowing the horse to create a miracle.

Horses can heal you from the inside out—they're very therapeutic.

This might be a good time for me to talk about therapy again for a moment. Many people come to me after seeing a professional therapist for years, and they say, "Wyatt, I've talked about my problems for my entire life and nothing has changed. What's the matter with me?"

Here's my answer: "Nothing."

I've been doing this for 20 years, and the longer I do it, the more I know that for some people, conventional therapy—one hour in an office and then your time's up—doesn't work. It's my opinion that after years of therapy involving a weekly appointment and a couch, it might be time to make a change. Do something different.

For those who haven't been in therapy, I point no fingers. One of the things that happens to people who have been emotionally damaged is that they honestly don't believe they can change their life or get rid of their pain. They've been operating out of this traumatized place for so long that it almost seems normal. But it's not really working for them. They need to change it . . . and they're not alone. The entire planet has been traumatized in one way or another. However, that's not an excuse to continue to be a slave to one's pain—it's just part of the deal until we change it.

I approach each person with the same message. A horse is consistent in his awareness—pure as he can be, totally sophisticated and always in the moment. A horse knows what to do every single time. It just depends on how clear *you* are as a human being. You have to be certain about what you're asking the horse to do. For instance, he won't lift his foot today based on how someone cued him yesterday. It's how you're speaking to him *right now.*

Sure, you can pet him until he's bald. Many others have tried, and he doesn't care. I've seen people walk up and coo, "You're such a pretty horse," while they just pet and pet him. But the horse moves away because he's paying no attention to the words and is sensing a massive amount of fear in the person. At this point, the horse backs off, as if to say, "Get the hell away from me. This shit doesn't feel right."

The horse moves away because that person's energy is cloudy, muddy, defensive, and unclear. It's like having a dangerous person walk up to you—you can sense it before the person even lays one finger on you. The overwhelming feeling is that something is wrong and you need to distance yourself from that person.

This "sense of feel" for living is one of the common threads we share with horses. It appears that we've used our heads to the point of losing our natural intuition, which is probably because we're so damn smart and are the most highly evolved of all the creatures on planet Earth. At least according to us.

The next part of this book will illustrate just how much we as humans don't know . . . but, if we're willing, can learn from horses.

⤬ ⤬ ⤬ ⤬ ⤬ ⤬

Chapter 8

v๑v๑v

Don't Talk, Don't Trust, Don't Feel

I'd like to take a little "time-out" here to tell you about unhealthy systems versus healthy systems. Unhealthy systems are closed, while healthy systems are open. Unhealthy systems also exhibit three common symptoms—don't talk, don't trust, and don't feel. In other words, don't be authentic. And when anybody decides to step out and heal, that unhealthy system will shake up entirely and fight to keep itself intact.

The majority of our systems are unhealthy. It doesn't matter what we call them: corporate systems, religious systems, or school systems—all are products of family systems, filled with people whose lives are hampered. However, at this point in time, we have an opportunity to look at how we can heal these systems . . . because we're seriously hurting.

Most systems are based on competition, so somebody will win and somebody else will lose. But if our main goal is to win, then the game becomes more important than the players, which prohibits closeness or connection with our fellow humans.

If we win the game, it doesn't necessarily mean that the heavens have opened up. Please. We won, they lost (or vice versa). End of story. I mean, do we ever actually feel good about those wins when we "get" the other guy? Of course we don't. The win is never enough—it generally means a short little rush, which is a lot like doing dope. The high only lasts a little while, the letdown comes, and we'll go out tomorrow hoping to win another battle so that we can have that feeling again. But we simply can't duplicate it every single day, so we end up feeling awful. It's a lose-lose situation.

The sad fact is that we set it up so that we lose no matter what happens. We've done this to reinforce the fact that we're flawed and there's everything to fear. But what if we as a culture confront our self-doubt and fear? That's what I'm trying to do every day with these horses—confront that fear and say that setting ourselves up to lose is bullshit and absolutely does not have to happen.

The next several chapters are firsthand accounts of how some people broke out of their self-imposed prisons and found the courage to confront their fears and move on.

Chapter 9

ငာ•ငာ•ငာ

Crackers Saves a Life

As I look over a 20-year practice, the story I'm about to tell is probably the most dramatic—and certainly one of the most heartwarming—examples of change in a human being that I've ever experienced.

Dennis was a 16-year-old boy who had already been dealing drugs as a means of supporting his own habit. His mother brought him to treatment because she was terrified that he'd gotten himself into a situation that could cost him his life.

At least on the surface, Dennis came off as cold, tough, and calculating—and it was even rumored that there was a contract out on his life. I took one look at him and just knew that this boy was full of rage and had gotten himself to a place where he truly didn't give a damn about any of the consequences that might befall him. Here was a kid who simply had grown up too fast.

Dennis stood out in the patient population—which took some doing, considering that we allowed these kids to have some freedom in their manner of dress (as long as it didn't promote drugs or alcohol and wasn't profane or vulgar in nature). In his bright-yellow pants cut off below the knee, red sneakers, and sloppy sweatshirt, he certainly wasn't someone who was trying to hide. In fact, he seemed to be saying, "Come over here. I'm just a kid. Please pay attention to me."

For the first ten days of treatment, Dennis tended to be very closemouthed and often looked like a caged animal. But at some point during the second week, he had wandered into the barn and was introduced to a beautiful Welsh pony/Arabian mixed horse named Crackers.

Somehow, this distant, angry boy let that horse in. The cold, caged-animal look would leave his face when he looked at Crackers and touched his soft mane. Whether he knew it or not, Dennis's healing had begun.

One weekend, I received a call at my home from the staff at the treatment center. It turned out that Dennis had pretty much taken over the unit he was living in. He was, in effect, holding the support staff and some of his fellow patients hostage.

By the time I arrived at the unit, he was standing in the middle of the room, where a nurse was trying to reason with him. The boy was in a rage, and every other phrase out of his mouth contained the word "fuck."

"Fuck this place, fuck the staff, fuck you!" Dennis

screamed. When he was aware that I had walked through the door, he looked at me and shouted, "And what the fuck do *you* have to say?"

"At the moment, nothing," I said in a calm voice. "I heard there was a problem and came out to see what was going on. Mostly, I just came to listen." I looked him in the eye and said, "Usually, when someone says 'fuck you,' it generally means they're either coming after somebody or they're going to turn and walk directly away. But you do neither, Dennis. You just continue to stand in the same place, saying the same thing."

Where this next question came from I have no idea. I heard the following come out of my mouth: "Does 'fuck you' mean 'help me' to you?"

Dennis's eyes seemed to soften as they welled up with tears. I slowly walked closer to him and said, "Could we go in the office and sit down and talk?"

"Okay," he whispered.

When we got to my office, I asked, "Can you tell me what's hurting?"

"My parents aren't coming to family week," Dennis spat out. And then he burst into tears. He had finally let me in. We talked further, and he gave me his word that if I would let him stay in treatment, he would stop holding people hostage and screaming obscenities.

Later that night, I was told that Dennis had gone down to the barn to spend a little time with Crackers.

A few mornings after this incident, during one of our daily staff meetings, hoofprints were discovered on the recreational field next to the stable that the kids had named "the field of dreams."

We went out to investigate the hoofprints, and quickly determined that the horse that made the prints wasn't wearing shoes. Crackers was the only horse in the barn who fit this profile.

As we looked at each other, we immediately knew who had let Crackers out. If a person hadn't been involved, Crackers certainly wouldn't have been back in his stall the next morning. We would have had to put out an APB on Crackers because he would have opted for wherever there was grass to graze and things to investigate.

Ordinarily, a stunt like this would have been brought up in the patient community meeting, where it would have been confronted and remedied—and there would have been consequences. However, we decided to leave this one alone.

During the remainder of Dennis's stay, we continued to see Cracker's hoofprints on the field of dreams. No one ever saw the boy leave his room at night, and we had an excellent security system. Meanwhile, Dennis continued to make progress in treatment. He started talking about his feelings, and all of those negative behaviors that appeared in the first two weeks had ceased to exist. And he even agreed to extended care at a halfway house after he left us.

I never heard another word about his life being in danger. It was as if there had been some sort of divine intervention on this kid's behalf.

A month after Dennis left for the halfway house, he sent us a letter. I also personally received a call from him. Dennis told me, "I know you knew it was me who was hanging out with Crackers late at night, and I want to thank you for not busting me on it. Crackers saved my life. I could talk to him when I couldn't talk to anybody else on this planet."

He went on to tell me that he was sending another letter that he had written to Crackers and asked if we would read it to him. I wish I could share these special words with you. But without this young man's permission, I wouldn't dare to do so. We diligently tried to find Dennis, and even searched for him on the Internet. I hope he's alive and well and continuing the spiritual recovery he started in Tucson.

In case this young man finds this book, I want him to know that Crackers is still alive and well. He's approximately 20 years old, and I suspect he would remember Dennis if he were to see him again. I know I will never forget either of them.

Nor could I ever forget that during a troubled boy's 16th year on Earth, a horse got through to him when nobody else could. Crackers saved this kid's life.

Chapter 10

~~~~~~~

Mission Control

The need for control is always based in fear. A perfect example of this was Cliff, a man who had a massive need to control everything in his presence. I met him at a couples' workshop, but I worked with him separately from Delia, his wife—because she had pretty much grown to despise him. Delia's animosity sprung from her husband's delightful habit of attempting to control every move she made, from what she wore to how she spoke. He even felt the need to monitor her whereabouts when they weren't together.

One day, while I had the rare opportunity to work with both Cliff and Delia together, I found out that he was afraid to let go of *anything* because he didn't feel safe in any part of his life beyond his work. Now, I didn't find this out by asking him—I actually had to put him on a horse facing backwards and give Delia the lead rope.

"Her task is to take you anywhere she wants to," I told him.

Rather than arguing and protesting, Cliff began to cry. It turns out that he'd been abused by his mother and grandmother—so to literally not have the reins in a situation, and to turn his back and put his faith in the hands of a woman, was terrifying to him. Even though he really did love his wife and wanted to connect with her, he was also afraid that she would end up hurting him.

But Delia was a strong woman, and she offered him the opportunity to access the childhood traumas he associated with his mother and grandmother. She was presenting him with an opportunity to heal.

That healing began on the back of a horse on a sunny fall day. Cliff's wife did not betray him. As she led that frightened man around the arena, making sure he didn't fall or even come close to falling, she actually became a source of safety for him. By the end of the morning, Cliff felt something more for his wife than just a sense of longing, which had been his previous definition of love. He now felt *trust* for her. The truth is, you can't really love someone deeply until you trust them.

But most important, a part of this wounded man's past had been removed from his present life, and as a result, the love he and his wife shared had the freedom to grow.

Chapter 11

∾∾∾∾∾

Case Study: The Angry Guy Shoves a Horse

Now I'd like to tell you about Vern, the special horse who is the master teacher of the herd. Vern is an extremely sensitive sorrel thoroughbred. Even though he weighs approximately 1,250 pounds, he has consistently exhibited that his heart is bigger than his physical body. And many years ago, he taught me something that I still think about to this day.

I was doing some work with Gary, a cocaine addict who had been abusing himself for a long time. Gary was one of the angriest people I've ever come across—he was just seething with rage. After I gave him in-depth instruction on how to treat the horse, Gary promptly forgot what I told him and went on automatic pilot. His intent with the horse appeared totally unclear as he attempted to move Vern by shoving him aggressively and then defiantly standing too close to him.

I told him repeatedly to change his behavior and to give the horse some room. But Gary continued to invade the animal's space, and then, to make it worse, he even reached up and jerked on the horse's halter. I informed this man that if he wasn't willing to modify his behavior, we'd have to stop working with the horse immediately.

Now Vern is one extremely patient horse, but that day, when Gary refused to listen to me, Vern intervened on his own behalf.

I'd never seen Vern react like he did at that moment. In a flash, he laid his ears back and bared his teeth like a rabid dog. If I hadn't moved in quickly, Vern would have done some serious damage to Gary. What's especially amazing is that this wonderful animal had never once behaved like that before, and he hasn't come close to doing so since.

Vern knew one thing: It was his job to be the mirror to this man's behavior, and this was one hell of an angry guy. Yet I knew something else: Most *angry* people prove to be *scared* people. They're in pain, and their anger is often a secondary emotion.

When clients arrive at the barn and are obviously agitated, my staff and I are extremely vigilant with our attentiveness. Behavior like Gary's happens more often with men than it does with women. This is because men tend to openly express their anger when their horse isn't cooperating, so they'll get into power struggles—mentally and physically—with the horse.

Imagine the obvious insanity of this one. We have a 180-pound man who has chosen to get into a physical struggle with an animal that weighs well over a thousand pounds. I often equate this with getting into a pissing match with a skunk: There's no doubt who the winner will be.

This power struggle often begins when the client isn't aware or doesn't believe that anyone's looking. But I can instantly tell from the horse's response when anger is present. Horses don't react well to anger and often refuse to cooperate, behavior that usually causes an angry man's energy to further escalate.

What becomes obvious here is that if the anger is a cover-up for pain or fear, then the man has given the horse a mixed message. He's not being authentic, hence the horse's response: *Get real or get lost.* But when we're able to tap in to what's underneath that anger, the horse generally cooperates.

On the other hand, when working with female clients, I actually try to encourage them to express their anger, because women aren't culturally conditioned to feel or display anger at all. Apparently, someone decided that an *angry* woman doesn't equal a *nice* woman.

Well, this makes me think of a great saying I once heard. This one came courtesy of Burt, a guy who was a driver at the treatment center where I began my recovery. He used to say, "Don't be nice; be natural."

Now, this certainly doesn't mean that if you access

your anger, you'll automatically cease to be nice. But you've gotta confront the fact that maybe, when you consistently deny what you feel so others won't be uncomfortable, you aren't being nice *to yourself.*

As a defense against their anger, I often hear women state, "But I was taught to be a lady."

Usually, my reply to this is: "Look at what they've taught you—you should disempower yourself by ignoring your true feelings and be someone you're not. Translation: Who you are is not okay. So, do you want to present who you really are or pretend to be someone you think people will like better?"

I've been on this planet for more than half a century, and I have yet to see a human being invent a version of themselves that's superior to the original. And much like horses, we humans don't enjoy hanging out with phonies either.

I believe that anger is a healing energy. It exists so that we might take care of ourselves. If we don't use it for this positive reason and decide to repress it, the anger will mutate into a monster named "rage." Repress it often enough, and rage develops into a condition that either implodes or explodes—and this tends to produce behavior that results in the intensifying of our pain. So when people appear to be afraid of what they call "anger," I find that what's really harming them is rage.

I encourage the women I work with to use their

116

anger—when they first feel it—as energy. Again, it's a healing energy, and it's there to help you. If you track it backwards, it will lead you to where it's coming from. Feel the anger. Energize yourself with it. But by all means, do not use the anger to harm another, and do not use it against yourself.

As for Gary the coke addict, he just didn't get it, even though he did end up surviving that afternoon at the barn. My prayer is that on some other day, he *did* get it.

Chapter 12

ᴗᴖᴗᴖᴗ

The Deepest Pain of All

Carmen, a woman in her early 50s, came to the Equine Experience a few years ago. You could tell that she was really closed off from the world—the emotional wall around her seemed to be made out of steel.

That didn't deter Vern, our master teacher. Let me just tell you that people love that horse, and there are pictures of him all over this country. For instance, a well-known journalist in New York City has an 8"x 10" glossy of Vern in her office because he touched her soul. There are all kinds of people who say that Vern saved their lives. He's quite an angel. In fact, he was trained as a jumper, but I've only gotten on his back twice in nine years. This special creature isn't for jumping—he's for healing.

Carmen, the woman at the center of this particular story, approached Vern, and he wasn't comfortable with her from the start. He's a very sensitive horse, so each time she reached for him, he flicked his tail and moved away, bobbing his head up and down in agitation. When Carmen tried to work with his feet, Vern refused to lift them up. She couldn't get one of his feet off the ground. It was obvious that this was because she was so blocked, but she stood there asking me questions that mostly had to do with theories about horses.

I tried to talk to her about what was going on with her emotionally, but she halted the conversation mid-sentence.

"That's not happening!" Carmen informed me. "I'm not willing to go there."

"Fine," I said, staying with her and trusting the process.

Carmen did get to groom Vern, but he never relaxed with her. He just kept moving around, yet she was still unwilling to "get" that any of this was about her.

But I'll give her this: She stayed in the arena. Yet when we moved down to the round pen, where we work the horses, she was barely able to work Vern because of all of her pent-up energy. Her body was rigid, her jaw was tight, and her movements were choppy and exaggerated.

As she began to work with Vern, he didn't once consider a walk or a trot, but immediately broke into a canter. I had to step in and slow him down, because she nearly blew the poor horse into a gallop.

"Step back," I told Carmen as I held Vern's halter. "He can't be going too fast in here because it's too small of an area. If his feet go out from under him, he could break a leg. And we want to protect him."

"Okay!" she snapped.

But I could see that this tough-as-nails woman was starting to experience some emotion. Her lip was beginning to twitch slightly, and her eyes would mildly tear up—but she would quickly think it away.

By this time, Carmen had given up working Vern without any type of conscious communication having occurred, and he finally gave up, too. She and I were at one end of a 60-foot round pen, and at the opposite end was Vern . . . who was just staring at her. Keep in mind that as a person relaxes, the horse will come in. Well, there was no way he was coming.

Carmen waited and waited. Finally, she said, "I guess he's just not coming."

I studied her and asked, "Do you miss connecting with other living things?"

She finally burst into tears.

"What's going on here, Carmen?" I inquired. "You've been so closed up since you've been here. I know this has been difficult for you."

"*Life* is difficult," she responded, crying harder.

It turns out that two months prior to coming to

the Equine Experience, Carmen's mother had died of cancer. And a month after that, her husband had left her for another woman. When she told me that part of her story, she collapsed against my shoulder, and I put my arm around her.

She was crying and whispering, "Oh my God. Oh my God." The pain was just pouring out of her.

All of a sudden, I heard a familiar noise. Vern had walked all the way across the pen, and he laid his head right across her shoulder and blew his breath in her hair.

Carmen jumped. "Jesus!" she practically screamed.

"It's okay. He just came over to support you." I told her. "Put your arms around him."

She put her arms around that horse and cried for the longest time. Even though Vern had a big wet spot on his neck, he didn't move. He just kept breathing into her hair.

When Carmen's tears had subsided, I said, "Look at what finally happened here. Vern was waiting for you to show up so that you could connect with each other."

This whole scenario was a wonderful example of how we can never hope to connect, experience closeness, or know love if we're not letting our energy flow. It's the fear of feeling more pain that's the major block to experiencing love. Carmen had every reason to be closed up but finally let herself relax and let go. If we aren't exposed to how to deal with pain (such as she did), we'll remain closed up and do whatever we have to in order to survive.

Most people are stronger than they know. Horses know that for a fact.

❦   ❦   ❦

The hope of healing is what brought Vanessa, a young woman who had been sexually abused, to a workshop I was facilitating. One of the things pointing to her abuse was her posture as she worked the horse in the arena. I've found, after years of working with abuse victims and seeing their body language, that the body never forgets and always tells the truth.

From her head to her waistline, Vanessa's body was straight and engaged with the horse. But from her waist to the top of her legs, it was a different story. She had created a break in the flow of her energy, which in turn didn't direct the horse to move forward consistently or smoothly. The power of "her seat of creation" had in effect been taken out of her energy transmission toward the horse.

As I watched this take place, I couldn't help but ask, "Is there a reason your body language is such that you've taken your pelvis out of the equation?"

"Maybe," she began, "but I didn't even realize I was doing this."

Vanessa went on to tell me of how she was raped at age ten by a "family friend." She had been in emotional and psychic pain over this for 25 years. She went on to say that her pelvic area was numb, and that she had participated sexually with her partners mostly out of duty and had never been able to experience any pleasure during intercourse. She seemed unable to equate sexuality with pleasure—and certainly not with love.

I asked Vanessa if she would be willing to do some specific work with the horse regarding this issue. We went on to talk about sexually abused women feeling as if they had been robbed, which was something she could certainly relate to.

"My body doesn't even feel like it belongs to me," Vanessa said sadly.

I shared with her that it wasn't the first time I'd been told this by a woman. Then I talked with her about her work being a "reclamation project." By this time, she was in tears and her body had begun to tremble.

I brought in two other female group members to support her, and then I asked Vanessa if she'd be willing to sit on the horse's back as part of reclaiming her body. She nodded. This woman had tremendous courage.

After we had the horse prepared and set up for Vanessa to mount, her fellow group members assisted her in getting on the horse's back. The next step was explaining to her how a rider communicates with the horse, which primarily has to do with signals from the rider's seat bones, pelvic area, and calves. I knew that in order to communicate with the horse, Vanessa would have to the make the decision to consciously feel with her pelvis.

I asked her to breathe deeply and to send the breath as directly as she could into her pelvic area. I asked her to allow herself—gradually and taking all the time she needed—to slowly feel the movement of the horse between her legs.

A multitude of emotions began to surface within Vanessa—large amounts of pain, sadness, and shame came from within her as we worked to separate her past trauma from the present time. While she worked through this, she fluctuated back and forth from being 10 years old to being 35. But, for the first time, Vanessa was able to work through some of the shame she had felt, and she was able to determine that none of this was her fault.

At that moment, she accessed an equal amount of anger, which resided at the opposite end of the spectrum from her pain and shame. I encouraged her to continue to feel the anger and use it to energize her entire pelvic area. At that moment, she was able to take instruction on how to use her seat bone and lower legs to move the horse forward. So much energy flowed from this woman to the horse that he almost started at a trot, but as usual, we had a competent horse handler to prevent this from happening.

We then began to show Vanessa how to work with the energy so she could consciously communicate with the horse. She was able to propel the horse forward at a walk, then a trot, and then back to a walk, turning him both to the right and the left. Then I told her that one of the ways to stop the horse was to employ the Kegel method (an exercise women are trained to do to help ease the pain of childbearing). You see, just by squeezing that area of the body, it transmits the need to stop to the horse. Vanessa did this, and the horse stopped immediately. She was laughing, crying, and exhibiting a sense of wonder.

Leaning down into the horse's neck, Vanessa whispered, "Thank you, thank you."

I encouraged her to close her eyes and say thank you to *herself* because she had been the one who had truly done the work. At this point, I asked her if she wanted to ride around the arena just for the joy of riding. "Oh, yes," she said and moved the horse forward.

Moments later, I asked her if there was anything she needed to say as she rode, to express her newfound freedom. Suddenly, she raised both hands into the air and proclaimed at the top of her lungs, "My vagina belongs to me!" By this time, six other group members, the horse handler, and I were all in tears. Once again, this strong woman shouted, as if to the entire world, "My vagina belongs to me!"

The horse, a ten-year-old Arabian named Adieu, had been there for the entire experience, willingly being of total service and support while Vanessa did her work. At no time during all of her emotional work did this horse even flinch.

The workshop concluded two days later, and Vanessa's transformation was stunning. Oh, by the way, afterwards, when she worked the horse in the arena, she stood straight as an arrow.

Chapter 13

ᴖᴖᴖᴖ

Sightless, but Not Handicapped

Years ago when I was doing workshops for Sierra Tucson, I led a group where one of the participants was Dorothy, a 50-year-old Navajo woman who was blind.

I had been asked by the people booking the workshop if it would be safe to have a blind person in the group. The first thing I thought of when I heard the question was what Jonas Irbinskas, my dressage teacher and mentor, had repeatedly told me: "Being with horses involves a sense of feel." Over the years, as I trained with him, I probably heard that phrase 1,000 times. "A sense of feel, a sense of feel . . ."

So when I was asked that question, I immediately answered, "Of course it's safe."

Dorothy was an absolute delight to be around. She certainly was *not* handicapped. Although she couldn't see with her eyes, she was far from being blind. She saw with her heart.

Once she got into the arena with the horses, Dorothy leaned her cane up against the fence and began to work from that sense of feel. It took her no time at all to get the horse's hooves done, and then she groomed the horse in an expedient fashion. In fact, she was the first one done and was all set to walk her horse before anyone else was even ready.

Later on, after everyone was finished, we went down to the round pen. That particular day, I was using Vern, who, as I've mentioned, is the herd's master teacher. As I was demonstrating how to move him from the walk to the trot to the canter with simple body language, something strange happened. Every time I would get him into a canter, he would drop back into a trot. When he did this, I started checking my own energy, wondering if I was present. I knew that horses always respond to humans' energy, so Vern would just be mirroring whoever was in the ring working him. But on this day, he went into the trot from the walk or canter without my doing anything. Suddenly, it was as if I wasn't even involved at all.

I began to notice exactly where Vern would drop into the trot. When I looked at where it occurred, it was outside of the ring, right where Dorothy was sitting. I began to watch her and then watch Vern. Every time he would go into the trot, she would smile.

All of a sudden, I got it. The energy was so strong from her that, as far as Vern was concerned, I was taken out of the picture. I stopped what I was doing and walked over to Dorothy. I asked her, "What's your favorite sound that the horse is making?"

She said, "This one," and demonstrated a fast "click, click, click" sound.

Well, it turns out that Dorothy loved the sound of the trot, and each time Vern got close to her, she "flipped his switch." It was the damnedest thing.

Sense of feel? I think so.

This was the first of two enlightening experiences I had with supposedly "handicapped" people. The second one occurred right after Miraval had opened.

Marty was a blind songwriter, and he and his wife had signed up for my workshop. Again, I got the same question: "Would this be safe for them?" This time, I didn't have to think about it for a millisecond.

So they came down, and once again, the blind person was the first to finish the grooming process. In addition, Marty was working with Sisi, the youngest horse in the barn, who was known for his restless nature. But on this day, as Marty worked with him, Sisi remained totally still.

The workshop progressed as usual, and we made our way to the arena. It was a small group that day, and at the conclusion of working the horses, I told everybody to try to relax to the point that the horses would sense it and just walk up to them on their own accord.

Sometimes this works, sometimes it doesn't. If the person can relax enough, the horse will "come in" to them, meaning that the horse will walk directly into the person's hands. But Marty had so much energy churning inside of him that I had to ask him to relax a few times. His energy was so intense that Sisi was almost airborne.

At first, this was a great thing. It was a piece of cake for Marty to get Sisi to work at the walk, trot, and canter; and he had no problem whatsoever turning the horse using just his energy. It was like he had been doing it for 100 years. The problem was getting Sisi to stop. When he was finally able to relax enough for the horse to put on the brakes, Marty got a little bit sad. Now it didn't appear that Sisi was going to walk toward him at all; he just couldn't relax to the point that he'd be inviting the horse in.

Keep in mind that this man couldn't see his surroundings—he had no visual awareness that the horse he was working with weighed 1,000 pounds. Given those facts, what happened next was quite remarkable.

"It's important for me to have the horse come over," Marty told me. "And I can't seem to relax, standing where I am."

"You're the only one who knows what's needed next," I responded.

Marty knew where Sisi was located in the arena, and he immediately sat down on the ground with his back to him. I had to trust that this was perfectly okay, so I stepped away.

I could see his body slowly relax. And as you might expect, after about three minutes, Sisi walked slowly toward him from behind. There was no doubt that this was safe. Marty held up his hand, and the horse licked his fingers. Slowly, he stood up, hugged Sisi's neck, and couldn't stop smiling.

Once again, it had been proven to me that life is lived in its most meaningful way, and at the deepest of levels, through a sense of feel. I have often looked back on those two experiences with Dorothy and Marty, remaining in awe of the type of vision that they possessed.

They were perfect reminders that things are never quite what they seem.

❧ ❧ ❧ ❧ ❧ ❧

Chapter 14

ᘒᘒᘒ

The Breast Cancer Survivors

I can't generalize about what "everybody" does when I offer them the opportunity to approach a horse—it's different each time. But people do tend to bring the same two things with them to the arena: self-doubt and fear.

Well . . . most people. A group of breast cancer survivors came to Miraval a little while ago. They were either in remission from, being treated for, or had been totally cured of, this horrible, life-threatening disease. All of these women had expressed the desire to attend the Equine Experience.

From the start, I was aware that I was in the presence of something truly phenomenal. When these remarkable ladies and I sat down in the group area (where I offer an explanation of what's about to take place), something happened that I had never experienced before.

There were approximately seven horses in the general vicinity of the gathering area, and all of them were standing at attention, with their necks stretched over the fence and their ears pricked forward. Their noses were pointing directly at the women.

I was both touched and amazed by what was taking place. As the women began to present information about themselves, it was plain to see what the horses had been attracted to. As I listened to these survivors, their stories revealed that every woman there that day had in fact experienced what spiritual literature calls "the dark night of the soul." That is, they had truly faced the prospect of death, looked it straight in the eye, and journeyed to the other side of their fears.

This group of women was totally in touch with what was important in their lives, and their priorities indicated the absence of games, surface talk, or anything else that would imply that they might be sleepwalking. And the horses were totally drawn to their authenticity—it was as if they knew that they were in the presence of some very special beings. When I suggested that the group look at what the horses were doing, one woman marveled, "Isn't that amazing?"

"Not to me," I replied.

When these women walked up to the horses and began to participate in the grooming exercises, everything was so easy for them. The horses cooperated with them as if they had just been reunited with old friends. I felt the same way.

This group and their particular struggle represents one part of the human experience. They were a perfect example of the duality of life's expression—that what appears to be a curse can oftentimes be a blessing. They remained at Miraval for approximately five days. Since then, on more than one occasion, fellow staff members and I have shared what *we* experienced by simply having the privilege to be in their presence.

We've occasionally had a breast cancer survivor come through our program since that group visited us, and the results have been the same 99 percent of the time. It consistently looks as if the horses have been reunited with long-lost friends, and I never cease to be amazed by this phenomenon.

ℭ℘   ℭ℘   ℭ℘   ℭ℘   ℭ℘   ℭ℘

Chapter 15

༄ ༅ ༄ ༅ ༄

The Formula for Change

This would be a good time to mention two constants that are always available each time I present the Equine Experience to people. I've already touched on the first one, which is the chance to speak the language of horses: energy. Horses are a simple, honest gauge of our energy and will reflect it right back to us. Through working with the horses, we can learn to tune in to what our true thoughts and feelings are and how that dictates our behavior.

The second constant is the opportunity for change. Horses can help us look at everything we've learned—from birth to the present moment—related to how we choose, enter into, and negotiate relationships. How is this possible? Well, when humans begin to work with horses, what tends to happen is that things don't always go smoothly, so we tend to make up a story about it. In other words, we *diagnose* the problem.

And once we've done that, we'll usually make it about the horse. Of course, it's *not* about them (which you might have gathered by now), but hey, since we're conditioned that way, we just keep doing what we're familiar with.

But we can try something a little different here. When we work with horses, they help reflect the areas in our lives that block us or bring us into conflict with ourselves and others. So, instead of making it about the horse (or somebody else), we can take the opportunity to change. Here's how.

Once we've seen what our problems are, we can ask ourselves how we normally deal with situations like the one the horse brought up. Now, if we've tried what we know and it worked, great. But if it didn't work, the opportunity for change has arrived: *Let's not do that anymore.* Next, we can try something different. But if *that* doesn't work, we can keep doing something different until we're blue in the face . . . or we ask for help.

So, to repeat: Try what we know—if it doesn't work, try something different and/or ask for help. If we'd only complete these steps, I promise that life will get easier. It's impossible for it *not* to.

There's just one problem with this formula: It appears that asking for help isn't part of our culture's awareness, nor does it seem to be acceptable everyday behavior. I have a theory as to how this happened.

See, for hundreds of years, we've been a patriarchal society, so not asking for help has been an unwritten rule imposed upon our culture by a bunch of scared men. Now that's all well and good, but it's time for us to stop blaming whoever created the rule. We've had plenty of time to confront and change it. In fact, over the course of my lifetime, I've noticed a shift in this attitude more and more. Men are now *allowing* themselves to be afraid, which gives them the opportunity, by the way, to *stop* being afraid.

Just as men aren't supposed to be afraid, women aren't supposed to be angry. Now, I've never met a man who wasn't scared, nor have I met a woman who wasn't angry. But our culture is resistant to change—we call scared men "wimps" and angry women "bitches." And whenever I question groups regarding what it means to ask for help in our culture, the answer is almost always unanimous: "It means you're weak or stupid." Therefore, in order to be seen as a strong, intelligent person, you apparently have to know everything.

Gee, I remember when *I* knew everything. How 'bout you? It's time to stop living in the world that's been created for us and create the one we deserve. If we need help, we should ask for it. But most important, we've got to stop sleepwalking and accept responsibility for our own lives. Horses can help us, but in the end, we've got to do it ourselves.

Chapter 16

ᑌᕋᑌᕋᑌ

The Issue of Responsibility

I had an 80-year-old woman in the arena one day holding the rear hoof of a 1,200-pound animal. She had never been near a horse in her life. "I never would've thought in a million years that I could do this!" she gasped.

"How many times have you restricted yourself?" I responded. "How many times did you say, 'I could never do that'?"

"Too many," she wistfully admitted, adding, "I guess whether or not I continue to do this is my responsibility, huh?"

It was a beautiful moment. Even at 80 years of age, she was pushing the envelope one more time. Just know that every time *you* do that, the entire world gets larger and becomes more exciting. But it's *your* responsibility to be make it happen and not just wait for things to happen to you.

This might be a good time to remember that shit happens. However, it doesn't have to be that way—you can avoid the shit by being responsible.

This responsibility also crosses over to all of our relationships—as friends, lovers, parents, co-workers, and as human beings in relationships with ourselves.

Five years ago, I met a 74-year-old man at the Equine Experience, and as a result of my interaction with him, I've quoted what he said to me almost every day since. I don't even remember his name, but that doesn't matter.

I was explaining what we were going to do in that afternoon's group, and halfway through my monologue, he stopped me cold and said, "Excuse me, son."

I had to smile, since at my age, it's rare that anyone addresses me in a fatherly fashion, but when I looked over at him, his eyes were very intense.

"Are you saying that I'm 100 percent responsible for 50 percent of every relationship I'm in—in other words, my half?" he asked.

"I *was* trying to say that, but I wasn't doing nearly as well as you just did," I responded with a grin. "Do you mind if I quote you?"

His reply was simple: "Well, you wouldn't be quoting me. I was taught this 12 years ago, when I was 62, and it changed my life," he said. (It was an extremely private experience that he didn't want to share with the group.)

I thought to myself, *This guy's another example that, regardless of your age, it's never too late to wake up.*

One way that our culture trips us up is that it hasn't conditioned us to look at responsibility rationally. When something goes wrong in a relationship, one person will tend to take *more than* their half of the responsibility for it. Self-doubt rears its head again, and people find themselves saying, "It's my fault that things went wrong. I screwed it up again." A lot of times you'll even have two people in the same relationship telling themselves that they're the screw-up. This is ludicrous, since this kind of behavior doesn't hold the other person responsible for a damn thing.

May I suggest an alternative? How about if you just take care of *your* half of the relationship? If you do that, then it's like you're saying to the other person, "I honor your intelligence, your capabilities, and everything about you. I know you can take care of yourself. You can handle your half. If you should want or need my assistance, just ask. I'll be there for you."

But if you assume responsibility for all that's problematic in the relationship, then what you're really saying to your partner is, "You're too stupid to handle your own stuff, so I'm going to do it for you."

People are pissed off all over this planet because that last way is how it often plays out. Culturally, women have been conditioned to receive this kind of treatment. But sometimes there's nothing worse than a co-dependent male who sweeps in on a white horse in an attempt to save the day . . . whether his partner wants him to or not. Men who behave in this fashion have been culturally led to believe that this is their job. When they "rescue," they think they're being loving. They're not. Bottom line: Your day doesn't need to be saved unless *you* think it does.

Instead of looking to the outside to solve an internal struggle, what if we all became responsible for owning our own power? Think about it. Wouldn't it be better to say, "I'm going deep inside myself to decide precisely what path I'm going to follow. It doesn't have a damn thing to do with what I'm *supposed* to do—it has everything to do with what excites me the most. And only *I* am responsible for whether or not this comes to fruition." Just by doing this, we could improve our relationships by 100 percent.

What generally prevents people from doing this is our good old pals fear and self-doubt. If we just deal with those two emotions, we can all self-actualize. It's that simple. And then we can ultimately take responsibility for every breath we take on this planet. The results will be stunning. Maybe we could stop wars, stop destroying the planet . . . and each other. But is this ever going to happen? I don't know.

I can only hope—but I have to believe it's possible.

Chapter 17

CACACA

Becoming Your
Own Parent

Doesn't it seem that it's become rather easy and almost common to blame our parents for every little problem we've ever had? I hear it time and time again: "Wyatt, I'm messed up for life because I had the worst parents on the face of this earth." This will automatically be countered by somebody else insisting, "If you think *your* parents were screwed up, well, listen to *my* story."

Both parties might have to take a number, because there seems to be an awful lot of competition for the "worst parents in the world" title. I don't want to sound harsh, but it's time to get past this once and for all. Yes, your mother was uncaring. And I'm sure that your father is still your basic nightmare. It's obvious that they liked your brother better (boy, do I know how *that* feels). But at a certain age, the real question becomes: "Now what are you going to do about it?"

Permit me to make a suggestion here: *Let's all get to a point where we become our own parent.* I came up with this concept after realizing that this is something that every adult on this planet needs to do. You see, I'd been doing some work with Brent Baum, a wonderful therapist in Tucson, who is the safest man I've ever been in the presence of in my life. Anyway, he developed a technique for resolving trauma called "Holographic Memory Resolution." Brent's work is truly remarkable, so I've taken some of his work and applied it to mine.

Okay, the first thing you need to realize is that *everybody's* parents made mistakes. The sad fact is that all of our neuroses subconsciously get passed down from generation to generation because most people tend to just mimic the same style of parenting that they saw in their own mom and dad.

Some parents say, "Oh, *I'll* never do that to my children." But you know what? Kids don't care what their moms or dads *say.* They care that their parents' *actions* remain with them—much like an internal tattoo of sorts. So unless a person looks at changing their internal landscape, they will indeed revisit the behavior of their parents on their own kids. Changing from within is the only way to ensure that mistakes don't get repeated.

Now, I know that we're talking about altering

deep, lifelong patterns, but if you work within a protected environment, it can be done. Understand that even as an adult, you still need a protector. I don't mean that you should call up your elderly parents and ask them to step back in and hold your hand. That's not their job anymore. *It's up to you.*

Think about it: People are walking around all over the place trying to solve the unmet needs of their childhood, conditioned to look for external solutions to this problem. Some people try to find a solution through their work; others travel from one marriage to another—but it never works. The need never gets met.

There's no external remedy for an internal problem.

Realize that if you're looking for something external, it *is* usually related to your childhood. The child is basically looking for someone to say, "You're okay. You're important. You're lovable." You have to go back in to where the wound is located, clean it out, dress it, reframe it, and let it heal. Only then can you move on.

Becoming your own parent begins with some self-realization. To start, you must allow yourself to look at the repeated patterns of behavior that don't work for you. More often than not, people sabotage themselves because they feel overwhelmed—which is usually driven by some sort of emotional injury or an event that got imprinted and keeps showing up.

So, when something goes wrong, it's as if a life

circumstance touches a spot deep inside you. Suddenly, you feel much younger than what you chronologically are at that moment. Sure, you're living in an adult body, but emotionally, you're a child again. Your partner rejects you and—*boom!*—you're back on the playground, where you were the last one to be picked to play soccer. Your boss overlooks you for that raise—*zap!*—it's third grade time again, when you were the only one who failed the big history test.

It reminds me of something I was told more than two decades ago: "Recover or repeat."

If you'd like to recover, take the time to offer yourself the following gift. When you experience emotional triggers, make mental notes of them. Now you might be in a situation where all you need to do is relax a minute and take four or five deep breaths; or you could even write it down so you may come back to it later. Wait until you've disengaged from the emotional charge of the trigger, and create some space to get quiet. Close your eyes and allow the memory to resurface. You should get a clear awareness of the age you're dealing with here. Look closely at what's going on within the memory. What are you feeling? Who's present? What's the particular event surrounding all of this?

Here's an example of what I'm talking about. Not long ago, I met Ed, a 50-year-old business executive who looked like he was about to crumble when his horse repeatedly backed away as Ed tried to brush him. This was clearly not the response of a successful adult male.

I asked this man, whose face was full of despair, "How old do you feel?"

With a shaking voice, Ed replied, "I'm ten years old all over again, and my dad is yelling at me. I can't please him in any way. That's how I feel with this horse."

"Okay, let's do something about this right now," I said. "Rather than going inside and re-creating the trauma, let's take that boy out of there. Close your eyes, Ed. Now, without losing sight of the kid, and with him still in your mind's eye, begin breathing yourself back into the present moment. When you arrive in the present, just nod your head."

It took about six breaths for Ed to come back to the present moment. Then I suggested that he bring this wounded part of himself into the arena with us. I asked him to nod again when this happened. When he had done so, and with his eyes still closed, I asked that he silently repeat the following to that little boy inside of him:

> *"From this moment forward, I'm your new parent. I'm your advocate. I'm your protector. And guess what? I'm living proof that we've already survived this once. I'm not*

going to judge you anymore or call you names. You're not stupid. You're not lame. You don't have to please me. Your job is to be a kid. You don't always have to get the job done perfectly. All of us use trial and error to learn anything we know."

We repeated this several times, focusing on the last sentence. As I reminded Ed, when we're kids, we're consistently told what our particular outcome needs to be, but we're never shown the map of how to get there. Due to this omission in instructions, children's perceptions quite often become confused, and their greatest fears are often based in lack of information or misinformation. But when you become your own parent, you have the opportunity to fill in those blanks.

Keep in mind that it's imperative to create safety for those wounded places. It can be done, and it's not just some sort of intellectual trick. You must be willing to feel the threat. I'm not saying that you should go back and dredge up all of the pain of your past— you already felt that hurt a long time ago. It's absolutely unnecessary to go back and traumatize yourself by re-experiencing the event. Just pull the child within you to safety, and rewrite your own script. You're making a new memory, because the old one is saying, "Watch out, it's going to happen all over again."

You've got to realize that the reason these painful memories exist is that during a trauma, a part of your psyche says, "I'm on overload. I can't fucking handle this. I'm out of here. Zing!" This is known as "disassociation," which is a defense mechanism to get out of that awful place during that moment. If you aren't equipped to deal with the pain, you'll go to another internal place, take the pain with you, and save it for later. And years after, when the psyche determines that it's safe to do so—*blip!*—the memory comes back.

If you don't deal with it at this time, the pain will continue to surface, even though you may become ever more sophisticated in your efforts to avoid dealing with it. You may find yourself indulging in compulsive types of behavior—such as overeating, gambling, excessive shopping, acting out sexually, or (like myself) drinking and doing drugs—to avoid experiencing any of this internal material. See, what you're doing here is trying your best to put a lid on the pain . . . again. But in the process, you'll actually end up creating more pain for yourself until one of two things occurs—explosion or implosion. And rarely will this occur when you're alone. It usually happens in relationships with other living beings.

Take the case of Amy, a 35-year-old teacher who came to Miraval one summer. She was scared to death to approach her horse. Standing ten feet away from the

153

animal in the arena, she was so afraid that she burst into tears. Slowly, I walked up to her and said, "It's okay if you cry. Please go ahead and cry."

Amy looked up at me, and through her tears, she actually smiled. Quite often, people just need to give themselves permission to be real. I was trying to give her that permission, and since I was her therapist, I happened to represent the parental figure.

Through her tears, Amy went on tell me a very sad story about her family breaking up when she was a little girl. Her mother and stepfather divorced when she was nine years old. Her brother wanted to stay with their stepfather, so the family got split apart further. Amy ended up moving 400 miles away with her mother, and she came to feel excessive amounts of fear and loneliness. At one point in her life, she had felt safe and happy—but now, everything had been completely turned upside down. To add insult to injury, a few months after their move, her mother was diagnosed with terminal cancer, and there was no one to take care of her but Amy. So, at ten years of age, Amy had to deal with the fact that she had essentially become her mother's parent. And then her mother died.

Look at what this girl lost in such a short period: By the time she was 12 years old, she had no mother, no father figure, and a brother who had become a stranger. She was rarely happy because she never got to be a child.

In the arena with the horses, I allowed Amy to be that child again. She could cry. She could throw a tantrum if she needed to. She could feel everything that she had to suck up years before in order to do a job she wasn't equipped to do.

When her tears finally subsided, I offered her some instruction on how to be her own parent. I actually went out on a limb and asked her something I rarely ask clients: "In this particular moment, how would it be for you to allow me to be your surrogate father?"

"That would be wonderful," Amy replied.

I said, "I'm just going to do this for a short amount of time until you get some idea of how it's done, and then you can begin the process of becoming your own parent."

In the process of our approximately 90-minute interaction, Amy was able to bring that ten-year-old girl back from her wounded place and say, "We've already survived this! Now I'm going to share with you how to *live*!"

She also told her traumatized child, "You don't have to put a lid on anything you need to feel ever again. I'll be right here. I'll hang out with you and share your tears, your pain, your fears, and your laughter."

Amy had moved from being stuck in the problem to being involved in the solution. And at the end of our session, her horse was cooperating fully, and she had new tears in her eyes—but these were tears of joy. She exclaimed, "I can't believe this!"

"Believe it," I said. "We both know what just happened."

What I was basically doing with Amy was trauma resolution, through the modality of looking at it as memory and then reframing it. But while we confronted her wounds, Amy made the decision to create a safe place for herself. She had truly begun to become her own parent that day, and I promptly resigned from the role.

It's important to note here that it isn't our responsibility to become some other adult's parent. I've seen these cases over and over again. You can't fix what's wrong with your buddy or your girlfriend or that nice lady down the street. They're scared inside, and they have to confront their own demons.

I've had people come up to me and say, "I hear you do good work. Do you think you might have a solution for me?"

"No, I don't," I say. "I've got some time, and I've got tons of support for you. I'll give you the benefit of any experience I have, but let me make it clear to you: *You* have the solution. I have the map, and I can show you where it is and teach you how to read it. But you have your own answers."

❧ ❧ ❧ ❧ ❧ ❧

Chapter 18

ငှာငှာ

The Ph.D. Learns
to Let Go

The best example I ever saw of a person finding their own answers happened with Brian, a young man who came to the Equine Experience. This was a brilliant guy who had never failed at anything in his life. He got straight A's in school, enjoyed an active social life, and had a bright future—in fact, at that time he was completing an internship to get his Ph.D. In addition, Brian had done a lot of work on himself and was really open in some ways. Yet, there was a part of him that remained totally closed off and very unhappy.

"I've been taught by other people for years, but I don't know *my* way." Brian explained to me. "Sure, I know how to read a book and take a test, but I don't know what to do with my life."

Now, one of the things I've learned over the years

is to trust what my gut tells me to do. Oftentimes what I'll be directed to do sounds absurd, but I've found that it's best to just go with it.

I had a hunch about what to do with Brian, so I told him and the eight other members of the group, "I need you guys to step out of here and go totally away because I'm going to set something up for all of us to experience."

My intuition led me to the far end of the horse arena, which was about three quarters the size of a football field. With my toe, I drew a circle about five feet in diameter, and I marked an X in the center of it. Nobody saw me draw the circle and the X, and it was way the hell away from where the group had been standing in the first place. So I brought the group back in, and I approached Brian with a blindfold, placed it over his eyes, and told him to stand in one tiny corner of the arena. Then I asked him to drape himself across the back of the horse, like he was a dead man.

"The truth is that for all practical purposes, you *are* dead," I told him, "and for right now, we see you as a damn corpse. If you're going to come back to life, you're going to have to access your source of truth, which is inside *you*—nowhere else. I believe you can find your way to a place in this arena that belongs only to you."

I asked a fellow staff member to hold the lead rope attached to the horse. "Okay, Brian," I said. "Your job is to find the spot with the X in it."

"But I'm blindfolded and lying across the back of a horse like a dead man!" Brian cried, obviously convinced that I'd lost my marbles.

"Everyone can see that," I told him. "But if you find the spot while blindfolded, you can never again say, 'I don't know what to do with my life.'"

I remember thinking, *This will either work or it won't, but whatever unfolds from this will be perfect.*

As Brian was lying on the horse with his eyes blindfolded, I placed two other group members on either side of him and told them, "If he starts to fall off the horse, for God's sake, catch him."

To Brian, I said, "Somewhere out here, in this vast arena, is your place in life. It's a circle, and when this horse has a hoof in it, you'll know it, and you'll tell whoever is leading the horse to stop."

And this articulate, well-mannered Ph.D. candidate said, "You've got to be shitting me!"

I shook my head, chuckled, and said, "No, I'm not shitting you—because *I don't believe that you don't know what to do.* I've never seen a human being who doesn't know what to do. I've seen people too damn afraid to make a decision, too afraid to go inside and look for the truth. So that's your task. We've got about two hours to find the truth."

To his helpers, I asked, "Everybody got sunscreen?" They nodded and lathered up. "Here we go!" I said.

The only way that Brian could steer his horse was by saying "right" or "left." He could also push on the horse's ribs with his hands, which dangled down on the side of the horse. Well, that young man went all the way down the side of the arena, and then he went back and forth across it a few times. And then, about 20 minutes later, he suddenly had the horse turn in a not-so-obvious direction.

I knew he was headed toward the spot. I felt it in my bones.

There was *no way* he could see the circle. He hadn't crisscrossed it in his travels—he hadn't even come 200 feet near it. The people walking the horse for him hadn't seen it either. But all of a sudden, Brian managed to bring his horse into that exact place in the arena that I'd marked.

"I think this is it," Brian said.

I said, "Let's get you off the horse and check if you're right." Meanwhile, the people leading the horse and protecting Brian started to cry. He got off the horse, and I removed his blindfold.

"Look down," I said. The horse had two feet inside that circle. "Welcome home."

Brian got it. He trusted his instincts to guide his horse to find that place.

I haven't done that exercise with another human being, but I'll never forget the look on that young man's face when he got off the horse and saw his circle. Brian, the buttoned-up Ph.D. candidate, burst into tears. He was in high joy. "I can't believe this has happened!" he cried.

I hear those words all the time. And here's how I respond: "Look at what has happened. You can't believe you're the source of your own truth? You can't believe you have the answer to every question you've ever had in your life?

"Believe it."

Chapter 19

༒

Love and All the
Good Stuff

Quite often, I spend time with people who are extremely critical of themselves for having multiple failed relationships. The truth is, they're missing the point: We *can't* fail, because there's no way to do these things wrong. A failed relationship, if you put it into its proper context, is a chance to either wake up or stay asleep, and it's what I refer to as an "AFGE"— or "Another Frigging Growth Experience."

If I had a dollar for every time I've experienced one of those, I could have retired 15 years ago!

For all the people I see who have been through horrible breakups, I encourage them to look at the Big Picture—which is "heal it or repeat it." Most of the relationship problems I've seen have been caused by the unhealthy relationships people have with *themselves*.

This is a good place for me to share a short, but true, story with you. A long time ago, a friend of mine told me something that stays with me to this day. He and I were having coffee when a man walked in who, by his mere presence, gave me an immediate emotional charge.

I leaned over to my friend and said, "I don't know what it is about that SOB, but I don't like him."

"How long have you known him?" my friend asked.

"I've never seen him before in my life," I spat, "but I don't like him."

He laughed and said, "Well then, Wyatt, it can't be about him. You have no history with this man. It has to be about you."

In other words, if you spot it, you got it. (It took me a few more years to figure out that this includes good qualities, too.)

Okay, back to the AFGEs. Marriage can certainly be an example of one of these. Let's look at what most people's idea of marriage is. Again and again, I've had married people say to me, "I thought my spouse was going to solve my problems."

The truth is, they're going to give *you* the opportunity to solve your problems. What a mate usually does is bring your problems right up in your face. They'll offer you the necessary discomfort so that you might wake up and become conscious, which will give you the opportunity to start the process of self-discovery. One of the things I can assure you of is simple: *If a marriage is going to be successful, there's always going to be some work involved.*

We seem to have bought into a generalized idea of what love means and how it plays out. Did you know that most people have no problems in the first three months of a relationship? There's even a select group who can *only* do the first three months. They're actually experts at it.

Well, who wouldn't want to be a specialist in this area? *Anybody* can do those first three months—after all, it's the warm and fuzzy, fresh and nice time known as the "honeymoon stage." This is where we get lost in each other's eyes and it's all roses and candlelight, as we maintain the illusion of a fairy-tale romance.

Then 'round about month four, somebody burps or farts. Oops! This thing starts to get real. Of course, that's no big deal in a healthy relationship. But for fantasy-based relationships, this is a *very* big deal!

Personally, I have a strong belief that the actual purpose of each and every union we make in this life is for healing wounds. More often than not, we're unaware of this, due to the fact that we've been conditioned to be externally focused in our relationships. This means that we spend the majority of our time wondering what others are thinking and feeling and making up stories about why they behave as they do.

But as long as we're doing this, it's impossible to be present in the relationship, so we really can't examine what's going on inside ourselves. Instead, we seem to want our relationships to fix whatever we perceive to be wrong with us.

Now, I have a problem with this whole "fixing" concept. In the first place, we're not broken—we're simply human. Of course we've got some sore spots, bruises, and wounds that haven't healed yet, but if we can just wake up, we can ultimately become our own doctor in these areas. I'm not talking about slapping a Band-Aid on the past and letting it fester for another day. I'm talking about really allowing ourselves to heal from the core of the internal trauma.

The more we can let go of the self-criticism, the higher the degree of healing will be. Only then will our relationships with each other improve, because love can't truly exist without self-awareness. Love is a *conscious choice*, whose genesis lies in basic respect for one's self.

So when we clean up the unfinished business in ourselves and in our family history, we can cut down on the AFGEs. Here's an example of this.

One day, Emily, a woman in her 30s who had devoted most of her time to building a successful career, came out to the ranch. She claimed to not have any problems . . . other than her inability to find the proper mate. As she put it, "All the guys out there my age are nuts. They're mama's boys who don't want to make a commitment, or they're cheaters and liars. Did common decency just skip an entire generation of men?"

It was obvious that she was looking in the wrong place for the answer to her dilemma. I asked, "How do you know these guys are nuts? And why do they keep showing up just for you?"

Well, it turns out that Emily had been engaged to a man in his late 30s who seemed like a really wonderful guy. But as the wedding date grew close, his behavior became erratic—to the point that he cheated on Emily with his ex-girlfriend, disappeared for two weeks, and then came back to announce that he was quitting his very lucrative job in advertising and rethinking his entire life . . . which at that point no longer included marriage.

I wasn't interested in delving into *his* deal. Instead, I simply asked her, "Has this happened to you before?"

Emily's eyes welled up with tears. She told me that when she was 12, her father ran away with another woman, and she didn't see him again until she was 20. From the time she began dating (at age 16), she repeatedly found herself in relationships with emotionally unavailable guys who would inevitably leave her.

And so, Emily had attracted someone into her life for reasons both logical and necessary. He was there so she might see her relationship patterns as an opportunity for change. Later, after her fiancé abandoned her, he got engaged to an old girlfriend—whom he subsequently broke up with a month later. Even then, Emily wasn't getting that *she* wasn't defective. But after our work, she had at least become aware of how her relationship patterns were setups for failure. She was able to see the work that needed to be done in order to break this vicious cycle, and to heal. And ultimately, she left us better equipped to at least cease choosing unavailable partners who would eventually abandon her.

Chapter 20

❧❧❧❧❧

The Journey of Anna and Daniel

At this point, I'm going to take a little break and let someone else do the talking. I want to hand you over to Anna, a bright professional who organizes retreats for the CEOs of some of the nation's top heath-care facilities. When she came to see me, the diagnosis was simple. She had one major thing missing from her life: love. Here's her story.

When I went to see Wyatt, let's just say that I wasn't the most optimistic person in the world. I was pushing 40, and although my life seemed to be going pretty well, one thing was missing. After a few particularly rough romantic breakups, I was convinced that there was no one out there for me, and my biggest fear was that I would die alone.

Of course, I didn't really have all the time in the world to dwell on my loneliness. I had to do my job, which is why I visited Wyatt at the Equine Experience in the first place. I was running a leadership symposium designed to restore the "heart and soul" of medical professionals, and I had invited 220 of the top cardiologists, health-care administrators, and CEOs in the country to stay at Miraval and experience the miracle of Wyatt Webb.

Before the conference was set to begin, about 15 of us from the group came in to meet with Wyatt and make sure we were all on the same page. From the start, I could only smile—because sitting in that corral, Wyatt wasn't the least bit intimidated by these highfalutin' doctors. I remember this one man who had a very fancy Yale education, but he couldn't get his horse's hoof up for anything. He actually began to push the horse a little bit out of frustration.

Wyatt went over to him and said, "So this is what happens when things get rough for you? You feel the need to push and shove?" The guy was immediately humbled, and he admitted that he indeed felt that he had to push or he'd get lost in the pack of medical professionals.

To another cardiologist, Wyatt joked,

"You've got so many degrees and little initials after your name, I don't even know what they mean. And this horse here doesn't seem to be impressed with how smart you are. All he wants to know is what you want."

Everyone burst out laughing, including the doctor.

One of the people who was laughing the hardest was Daniel, the CEO of just about the largest health-care system in the world. I had known him for about a year and a half, and he certainly was warm and friendly and handsome. But that's where it ended for me. At that time, my heart was almost completely shut down, so I'd always dismissed Daniel from my mind after our previous meetings. But I have to admit that on that cool winter day in Tucson, my stomach was doing flip-flops the moment Daniel entered the corral. Of course, I kept this to myself, because what was the point? Relationships just never worked out for me.

When we began working with the horses, I sensed that Daniel was giving me shy little looks, but I mostly ignored him and focused on brushing the horse. When I was sure he didn't notice, I'd give him a quick glance and then immediately go back to the task at hand. At the end of the hour, Wyatt pulled me aside and said a few words that I'll never forget.

"Anna, would you quit fucking around and tell that guy what you're feeling? It's all over both of you that you're connected," he said.

"Wyatt, I've barely even looked at him since I've been here," I lied.

To which Wyatt retorted, "I have a feeling that you've been avoiding relationships and commitment all your life. I repeat: Just tell this guy what you're feeling."

Now, Wyatt did not say the same thing to Daniel, who was working with the biggest horse in the pen. I remember that this horse immediately lifted his hoof when Daniel asked for it, but then something strange happened. Daniel dropped the hoof.

Wyatt approached him and quietly said, "So, Daniel, how often in life are you handed something that you let slip right through your fingers? Is there something in you that doesn't think you deserve what you're offered? I want you to look around this corral today—is there something of great value in here that you think you're not worthy of? You seem to be the kind of person who's always looking out for everyone else and forgets to take care of himself. Ask again for the hoof, but this time, hold on to it as if you deserve it."

As for me, happiness was also out of my grasp. Part of the reason I avoided love is because I was always in breakup-transition mode. It was my pattern to leave the men I dated for one reason or another, which obviously created pain for me. However, the pain became deeper two months before I came to Miraval, when I received the results of an abnormal mammogram. It completely traumatized me. I went through the biopsy alone, not even telling my friends and family what was happening because I didn't want to burden them.

The loneliness of this time was almost physically suffocating—even though, thank God, the health tests all turned out to be normal. But the experience was a wake-up call. It was as if a voice inside of me started to scream, "I'm going to be 40 very soon, and I have no one to to share my life with. I'll probably be alone for the rest of my life!"

That day in the corral, I told Wyatt about my fears. When I talked it through with him, I felt lighter as each word escaped my lips. It was as if I were tossing these fears into the dust underneath the horses' hooves. The fear and self-doubt were leaving my system, tossed into the earth and blown away by the wind. Wyatt listened, prompting me from time to time to tell him more. When we were through, I was crying and hoping that Daniel couldn't see.

"Anna, part of you has created your own loneliness," Wyatt said. "But this ache in your heart can disappear—if you want it to. The simple fact is that it's hard to attract someone of worth when you send off this vibe of fear across the room. You need to break that wall down."

I felt like I was having a deep spiritual and psychological experience that went to the core of who I was as a human being. And when Wyatt and I finished talking, I went up to Daniel and told him that I had always liked him and maybe we could spend some time together over the next few days. He told me that he felt the same way but always got the impression that I wasn't really interested in him. What a wonderful surprise!

I know that Wyatt would be embarrassed to hear me say this and I hope he doesn't take it out of the book, but I believe that he has a gift to give humanity. There's no better time, given current world events, for us to have someone like him because his healing has a ripple effect. In fact, I think all our world leaders should stop by the Equine Experience and go front and center with Wyatt and his horses.

Of course, I can't end my story without telling you the best part: Daniel and I are getting married soon, and I've never been happier or more at peace.

Chapter 21

ᦒᦒᦒᦒ

Helping Yourself

I am often asked what people can do if they can't make it to the Equine Experience—maybe they can't afford to come to Arizona or don't have the time to travel. Well, it just so happens that I do have a simple formula for helping yourself.

Look at the relationships you're in—whether they're easy, difficult, abusive, supportive, or loving. Really examine the dynamics of what's going on, and then ask yourself one question: *How am I positively contributing to this relationship?* Sometimes you'll discover that the only way to find that out is by asking another question: *How am I negatively contributing to this relationship?*

You see, as long as you remain a victim in any relationship, you're never going to empower yourself to walk through the pain. Children are often truly victimized, but adults actually seem to volunteer for this role. I know that sounds harsh, but it's true. As adults, what often keeps us in a bad situation is fear, misinformation, or no information at all.

Now if you want to wake up, you need to realize that you have the *freedom of choice.* You're making choices every moment that you're alive, and as a result of each choice made, one of two things will generally happen in varying degrees of intensity: You'll either get a reward or you'll get a consequence. This is because we live in a universe of duality.

Know that if you can become responsible for your own choices (rather than making them about someone else), then you can become responsible for your *life.* Nothing will ever change as long as you continue saying, "Look at what *you* did to *me.*" If that's your mantra, and you're choosing to wallow in the unfairness of it all, please be advised that while you're doing this, you aren't doing one thing to actually solve your problem. So, congratulations! You're stuck. And you may have set up a long wait, hoping that he/she/them will soon change so you can feel better. But even if *they* do, *you* won't.

Okay. Now that we've got that out of the way, keep in mind that the first step in coming to awareness is realizing one simple truth: *You must heal this or you'll repeat it.*

Perhaps you've wondered why people who have been battered tend to stay in abusive relationships. Well, sometimes they're afraid to leave because they're deeply afraid that they won't survive. It's the fear itself that keeps them in limbo. Many of these people need professional help, and they certainly need a lot of support from others; but the bottom line is that people in abusive situations need to feel safe enough to reach inside and say to themselves: "I have chosen to be in this situation for some reason, and it's not because I'm defective."

Remember that it's about being *100 percent responsible for your half of the relationship.* If that relationship is abusive, then you might want to consider that this probably isn't the first abusive relationship you've been in and that maybe you find yourself in this situation again because you're trying to work something out internally. In other words, your spirit is once again trying to heal—are you going to let it?

I often meet with people who say that they're hanging on by a thread emotionally. They feel totally overwhelmed. My heart goes out to them, and I want them to know they're not alone.

When we work through the emotional triggers related to past traumas, it will often evoke feelings of being hopeful—but at the same time, it's scary. When we experience our emotional triggers, we're often transported into a form of trance, which is what trauma memory is—it's about when we're passing through the world unconsciously. This means that we're not in "present moment time," which is the only time living is possible.

(For more help with this, I suggest that you pick up Brent Baum's book *The Healing Dimensions: Healing Trauma in Body, Mind, and Spirit* [available from his Website: **healingdimensions.com**]. Here, Brent expertly writes about this entire process of healing trauma, and rather than my trying it explain it to you, I think it would be more helpful if you just read his book.)

If you're having a tough time in life, join the club. *All* relationships consistently give you opportunities to resolve difficulties. If you're miserable in your union, the knee-jerk reaction might be "get out of here." But that's often not the solution—many times, you should stay.

As for myself, I know that some of the toughest relationships I've been in during my life were actually opportunites to learn something and heal. Except that rather than choosing to heal or learn and avail myself of the opportunity to take responsibility for my half of the relationship, I made it about the other person and then promptly went out and repeated the damn thing once again because I just didn't get it.

The point is, we're destined to get it. Sooner or later, our spirit is going to insist upon it. So deal with your resistance. You're here to learn these lessons, which you signed up for in the first place. It's the greater part of the human experience.

Now then, let's talk about the human experience for a moment. I strongly believe that when we connect with each other, we become the ultimate self-help group.

This is a fortunate time to be alive, although I know that with recent tragedies, a lot of people don't believe that anymore. Just keep in mind that since we live in a universe of duality, we're naturally going to experience some really tough times. But let's try to look at the possibilities at hand. There are so many opportunities for us to help each other—for example, September 11, 2001, certainly brought us an incredible amount of pain, grief, and suffering, but it also brought us a monumental opportunity for awareness. We have the unique opportunity to assist each other in a process of healing and unity.

Once again, we've been made aware of what's important to the human spirit. Sure, we've made great advancements in technology, but now we know that that isn't the answer. There's more affluence on the planet than ever before, but that isn't the answer either. Yet, as I look back over the last several decades, I'm excited about what we've had the opportunity to experience and learn.

It started in the '50s, with a misguided effort to change the consciousness of the planet as a result of that Ozzie and Harriet mentality of, "Here's how it's done. Let's keep it this way. Don't dare take a chance." That experience quite often translated into stagnation. We were complacent and were told to be happy with our simple lives, but we were very much in denial then (as we are now). It wasn't "simple" or "the good old days" for me or for a lot of people I knew back then. The good news was that the consciousness was about to change and we could no longer be satisfied with the '50s.

So then the '60s came, with all the disenchanted screaming, "Fuck it. This ain't working. I'm unhappy." We had some good ideas, but we also found some pretty misguided ways to go about "changing the world." For example, we began to ingest whatever was available in an effort to alter our reality. We appeared to be very much out of balance and a lot of the so-called ah-ha moments got lost in a drug-induced fog—which, of course, didn't allow us to ever satisfactorily integrate any of the wonderful ideas we came up with.

In latter decades, the process of change became evident in the country's behavior. In 1986, I was privileged to be a participant in an event known as "The International Prayer for Peace Breakfast." On New Year's Eve morning, every continent in the world chose a simultaneous time for worldwide prayer. In Nashville (where I was living at the time), it was 6:30 A.M. I took a treatment center full of kids to the breakfast, while millions of people across the globe gathered their own groups together. All the people of the world were praying for peace at the same exact moment. The energy was incredible—Buddhists, Muslims, Christians, Jews, and indigenous peoples from all walks of life turned up the volume knob of positive energy for our planet.

Look at what's happened since that morning in 1986. The Cold War ceased to be in existence. The Berlin Wall fell. Some of the more oppressive cultures in the world started to fold and change and began to allow their people the freedom of choice. All this happened thanks to an expression of energy from the everyday souls walking the planet.

Hands Across America was another event I was fortunate to participate in. I remember that day so clearly. To be standing on a rural road in Tennessee, singing my heart out with God knows how many other people hooked up to me, felt so powerful and life transforming. There were helicopters flying overhead filming all of it, and as I looked to my left and to my right, people were singing through their tears.

The transformation continues. People such as Oprah Winfrey are using the mass media to talk about things such as "remembering your spirit." When Oprah began this segment of her show, it shook up the system, and that frightens people. Even though Oprah was criticized in the press repeatedly, she's still doing it—quite successfully, I might add. I'm told that this comes from a pure place of conviction in her.

And in my little corner of the world, people are traveling thousands of miles to participate in this thing called "the Equine Experience." Corporate systems are inviting me to work with them to enhance the quality of people's work lives. This is one of the things I wrote in my personal mission statement years ago, when I laid out where I wanted to take this process.

It's so incredible to me that these large companies are taking the time to work on the *real* bottom line, which is the people in their midst. I'm presented with the opportunity to bring horses in and offer these companies the chance to begin getting honest and confront their fears. And I get to ask them, "Is what you're doing working or not?"

I had an extremely rewarding experience recently when I worked with one of the most prosperous companies on the planet, who had the foresight and awareness to realize that addressing the needs of their people in an honest and compassionate way is going to further enhance their prosperity. It's actually giving *them* an opportunity to remember their spirit.

I smile when I experience these corporate giants inviting some guy from Georgia (the one raised two doors down from the Baptist church, who spent half of his life fucking up everything he possibly could so he could find out what life was about) and giving him the chance to help them. Look at the magnitude of that energy and how it could conceivably change the world.

I know it's possible.

Evolution is slow in our time frame, but if we can take these opportunities, nurture them, and allow them to unfold, then God only knows what the outcome of that will be.

The garden has been planted. The question is, how are we going to be responsible for our half of this relationship? Are we going to fertilize it, water it, and allow it to grow? Is this some sort of pipe dream, or hippie woo-woo thing out of the '60s? Absolutely not. It's actually a spiritual principle in motion, and the masters have been talking about it for centuries.

✺ ✺ ✺ ✺ ✺ ✺

Chapter 22

High Joy and the Universe

I look back and am truly grateful for the opportunities I supposedly blew in my life. I feel particularly blessed by the music executives who wouldn't take the call of a drug addict and drunk. If I would have signed that record-company deal and made millions, I could also have wound up dead.

I can look back now and say with a grateful voice, "I'm so glad it didn't happen."

"It's weird how things work out," someone will say to me when they hear my story.

"It really isn't," I reply.

No, it's not weird at all. It's natural. The sad thing is that when the universe is cooperating and giving us everything we might possibly hope for, then we call it "weird." It's too bad that we aren't yet awake enough to see the order of it all.

Many years ago, in my own quest to wake up (I'm still about 95 percent asleep, let me make that clear), I read this book by Napoleon Hill called *Think and Grow Rich*. In that book, the author talks about how the universal principle governing money is exactly the same as the universal principle governing love. Basically, you have to give it in order to receive it.

So, I've told people who are worried about going broke, "If you're worried about having no money, go give some of the little you have away."

"That's the craziest thing I've ever heard of! Are you out of your mind?" they shoot back at me.

I understand that they think it's crazy. Naturally, you might think that if you only have a little bit of money, you need to horde it like a squirrel protecting her nuts for the winter. But see, the universe isn't set up to honor our fears and sense of lack. That's why, even when my funds were low, every time I passed one of those Salvation Army kettles at Christmas, I'd make a point of contributing something. It was often for no reason other than I always felt better afterwards. I promise you that the gift always came back to me. And the universe doesn't take long in doling out the rewards. There is just no way for this *not* to work. It's the law.

Let me share an example of this with you. Recently, Carin, my wife, decided to go back to school, and it required some unforeseen expenditures on our part. This created the illusion of money difficulties, and we worried about it together. Since this is the most conscious relationship I've ever had in my life, we were able to look for the solution together, which was nice.

So, on a trip to Walgreens one day, Carin and I were discussing our financial concerns. Upon arriving at the store, we saw this homeless man sitting out front on a wooden bench, playing guitar through a tiny amplifier. I'd seen this guy before, and God, could he play. Since he was obviously so talented, I told myself that something tragic must have happened in his life—but of course, I had no way of knowing if this was true.

Anyway, the first time I heard him play, I gave him five dollars. We talked a little bit about the blues—which was (appropriately) his favorite genre of music. Weeks later, I returned to Walgreens, this time accompanied by Carin. I had told her about this man and pointed him out to her. "There sits the guitar man I told you about," I said. All of a sudden, I felt ashamed to be worrying about money, especially since we pulled up to the store in one of our two black Volvos.

As we were talking, I thought to myself, *How dare I worry about money when that man doesn't even have a place to live and I have two Volvos that are paid for?* I reminded myself that I've never had money problems—only fear problems.

It was as if Carin had read my mind. "Do you have any cash?" she said. I didn't have any on me at the time. "Let's get some," she said. "Let's give him $20."

She was right (and quite often is, I might add). We went inside to pick up my prescription, and using my debit card, got an extra $20 to give to the guitar man. When we got outside, I handed him the money and said, "Happy Fourth of July."

"Hey, that's wonderful," he said, smiling. "Thank you!" His eyes sparkled, and he asked, "Do you know of any musicians? I'm looking for a band."

What he said suddenly put me in touch with how I had once sabotaged my own life. Music had once been such a big dream for me, and seeing this man's desire for something he didn't have from that business touched an old wound in me.

I said that I didn't know any musicians, and he smiled again and said, "I guess all I can do is never give up."

"I really wish the best for you," I told him.

"The same for you," he said. I sat back in the driver's seat of my Volvo, and at that moment, I felt a little screwed up. Tears came to my eyes, and I couldn't start the car. Carin said, "He really gets to you, doesn't he?"

"Yeah," I said. "It really breaks my heart to see somebody that gifted living on the streets."

Then Carin said, "We have no idea what lesson he's here to learn." She and I went on to talk more about how this man reminded me of my own journey. We hoped that maybe we had brought something positive into his world—as he most assuredly had to ours.

A few days later, I received a call from some people whom I had previously done some work for. From out of nowhere, they offered me one day's work in Dallas, which covered the tuition for Carin's school. But to me, it was a call from the universe, which keeps a running ledger on cause and effect. Do I believe that all that energy around our encounter with the guitar man and the $20 we gave him had something to do with it? You bet your ass I do.

It was like the entire universe was saying, "We'll give you an opportunity to create some abundance for yourself. Let's see what you've got!" Of course, as usual, I had some help from angels — one named Carin, and the other whose name I don't know, but who was sitting on the bench outside of Walgreens with a guitar in his hands.

I hope something good happened to the guitar man with his $20. It has to be so. It's the law.

∞ ∞ ∞

I've got a similar story about a woman who worked at my neighborhood grocery store in Tucson. Let me just preface this by saying that I hate waiting in line. I'm terrible at it, but I can do it better now because of her.

One day I was standing in the checkout line, and I heard this sunny, cheerful, almost buoyant voice say, "Good afternoon!" This woman was approximately

5'1" and not petite, was having a bad hair day, and would never be considered by our society to be a looker. But to me she was absolutely beautiful.

She looked people in the eye and said, "How are you today?" And she meant it. She wasn't the least bit invasive, merely genuine. Like my horse friends that I've told you about in this book, this gal was broadcasting a pure intent to connect with her customers.

She had supports on both wrists from banging on the keys of the register. It appeared that she might have carpal tunnel syndrome, which causes intense amounts of pain in the fingers and wrists due to repetitive motion. Yet, even in the most ordinary of life's circumstances, she was an abundant expression of pure joy. It was showtime in the checkout line!

Her happiness should have been contagious, but people passing through her line seemed uncomfortable. They'd stare at their feet, look to the left or right, rummage in their purses, do most anything they could to avoid her gaze. As for me, I couldn't keep my eyes off her. Although her line was longer, I stepped out of the short one I was in because I wanted to hang out and watch her. When she told somebody to "have a nice day," you could just feel that she damn well meant it.

By the time I placed my purchases on her conveyor belt, I was stoked. I was asking myself, *Damn, who is this person?* I was feeling so good when she looked at me and asked, "So how is your day today?"

"I want you to know something," I told her. "My day has been vastly improved by merely being in your presence."

"I just love my job," she said. "I get to meet so many interesting people."

Then she went back to talking about my day. It was as if she took what I said to her, allowed it to register deep inside, and it added another happy molecule to her already all-there, all-together, all-radiant self. I paid her, and she said, "Next time you come back, come to my register."

I did just that for some time, but one day I walked in the store, and she wasn't there anymore. I don't know where she went and I didn't even ask. However, for those moments in time, I was in the presence of someone I will never forget.

❧ ❧ ❧

One of the things I became aware of as a result of my encounter with that lady was that we don't have to be front-page news to add to the joy quotient of the world. Here was a woman in the middle of a grocery store who was totally supercharged and passing out kindness to whoever was willing to take it. What I found sad is that many folks were afraid of what she was offering, and some looked at her as if her high joy was odd. Maybe she mirrored to them what *wasn't* going on in their lives.

The guitar man and the checkout girl were reminders for me that a gift is always at hand—you just have to look around. There are so many people who walk through our lives who remind us of this fact . . . we simply have to pay attention to them.

Horses are reminders, too. They're carriers of the message, and they will neither argue with you about the message nor try to force it on you. They just keep saying in their way, over and over again, "What do you want from me?" And they sit there through all kinds of bullshit, just waiting for us to discover what that something is.

I need to tell you that I've seen some wonderful things here in Arizona. One of the reasons I love it here so much is that there's a powerful energetic presence all over this area. At the risk of sounding woo-wooey, there's an *expression of spirit* here. But that same expression lives in the middle of Chicago and in the middle of Trenton, New Jersey. It's everywhere.

It's even in that little Georgia town where I grew up, somewhere on the flip side of self-doubt and fear.

∽ ∽ ∽   ∽ ∽ ∽

Epilogue

M ore than 20 years ago, I was taught how to do something different. And several years after I learned that lesson, I was finally able to put it into practice regarding a highly sensitive and difficult matter—my relationship with my father.

You see, much of my young life (even prior to my alcohol and drug addiction) was spent lamenting over, and being angry about, our relationship. It took me six years in recovery and private therapy to resolve this matter, and I finally wrapped it up during a weeklong workshop in Chattanooga, Tennessee.

I was there with a group of eight other people, working on resolving the pain of the past. On the fourth day of the workshop, the facilitator set up an exercise that involved my writing the most painful details of my life down on paper. Then I was supposed to read them to the group and to an empty chair, which would represent my father sitting across from me.

For years, I'd been trying to identify, on as deep

of a level as I could, the pain associated with my relationship with my dad—but I could never access more than two or three tears at a time. It seemed as if I had an automatic shut-off valve that would spring into action every single time I tapped in to that pain.

This particular day, however, was going to be different.

As I began to read my information to that empty chair, surrounded by the support of my peers and a very competent therapist, I felt a degree of pain that I hadn't even known was possible. All of a sudden, as I read, I dropped the paper and began to spontaneously express the depth of my anguish.

The feelings were so intense that streams of tears were pouring out of my eyes, so I'm sure I must have sounded like I was talking underwater. But after what seemed like an eternity of purging, it suddenly ended with a voice coming out of my mouth, which was totally instinctive and not planned in any way.

Here's what I said: "And in spite of all this, Dad, I want you to know that everything is forgiven."

At that instant, the pain was over. I looked around the room, and everybody in the place was crying—including the therapist. I took a deep breath, and the valve was shut on that affliction for good. And then, I experienced a sense of relief and exhaustion that I believe is similar to what a mother feels after giving birth (even though I hope you understand that I could never even pretend to have the slightest inkling of what *that's* really like). I left the workshop feeling totally unburdened but wondering if what I'd accomplished would stick. You see, I wasn't accustomed to having things completely resolved.

My father never knew about this day, and as far as I was concerned, he never needed to. It wasn't his issue—it was mine. But about three weeks later, I decided to make the trip to Georgia to see my parents. I was a little apprehensive about this visit, but after arriving, having some food, talking about the Atlanta Braves, and getting caught up on who in town had died, I got bored.

I decided to take the opportunity to go outside and wash my car. When I began, my father came out and sat down on the porch. He did what he was famous for, which was pointing his index finger and saying things like, "Wyatt, you missed a spot over here."

But this time, I felt no emotional trigger. The therapy? Well, it had stuck. I suddenly started laughing, to the point of falling backwards into a puddle of water.

Dad looked at me with some concern and asked, "What is it, son?" I told him that he had no idea of how many times he had pissed me off over the years by "supervising" what I was doing or offering his unsolicited advice.

He replied, "Well, son, I was just trying to help. We don't get to see you that often. And I just wanted to come out and be with you."

I knew this was the truth. Shortly after this exchange, I realized that despite being the expert mechanic he was, my father's emotional toolbox was empty—but mine wasn't. So I decided to get to know my father. I was 41, and he was 77.

I asked him about his religious life, which, it turns out, gave him much peace. I asked him about his childhood dreams. Funny, but it turns out that a lot of the stories I made up about him weren't even close to being true. For instance, I had seen him as a tragic figure who didn't actualize his dream of a baseball career. But he told me that when he was a kid, he found himself in a blacksmith's shop and watched a man work with metal. From that moment on, he wanted to have his own machine shop. It turns out that Dad had, in fact, exceeded his dream, for not only did he have his own shop, but he was in charge of the biggest one at Burlington Industries.

I taught my father to hug when he was 77. Prior to that, we would part ways by shaking hands—because that's the way men did it. But on this visit, when I started to leave and he offered me his hand, I said, "We're not going to do it that way this time."

I took him in and hugged him. The best he could do that first time was pat my rib cage with his hand and laugh nervously. But by the second time we hugged, he had become an expert. His big ear pressed against my head, and I could feel his expression of affection. My father and I finally had a relationship with each other.

The last time I saw my dad alive, he'd lost the use of his legs. I was visiting, but I needed to be getting back. I started to leave, and he tried to get up from his chair, but his legs wouldn't hold him, so he fell back on the sofa.

I saw this out of the corner of my eye and said, "Maybe I don't need to go just yet."

I sat back down beside him on the couch, and all of a sudden, I found myself stroking my father's back. He had his left hand on my right knee, patting it. He was looking ahead like someone hypnotized, but he was smiling. Eventually I left, and my mother later called me up to say that when I'd pulled away in my car, my father had cried like a baby.

She said, "I haven't seen your father cry like that since he used to drink." So she asked him what was wrong, but he wouldn't tell her.

Later, I called my father and said, "I understood you had some tears."

"That's not like me," he said.

"So, what was that about, Dad?" I asked.

He didn't answer me on that one.

My father and I never did get really close—we just got as close as we could. The day he was buried, I had a picture in my wallet of the first horse I ever bought, a beautiful Arab named Heartwind. I was standing in the funeral home and I suddenly remembered that photo. When nobody was looking, I walked over to the casket and slipped it into my father's breast pocket so that he could take it with him. I had some understanding of his connection with animals, and this was my way of giving him something for the road.

My mother is 84 and still lives in Georgia, not too far from that little town where I was raised. By the way, she still thinks I'm perfect.

☙ ☙ ☙

Jarrod, my son, turned out to be quite a success story. He's very gifted musically, can play anything with a string on it, and sings like a bird—and he's certainly talented enough to have had a career as a songwriter. He's had people in the music community interested in him—but he checked it out for himself, saw the insanity of the business, and said to me, "I don't want any part of this stuff." He walked away from it. Currently, he's involved in the arts as a sculptor and owns his own business—a foundry that casts and finishes bronze sculptures.

It didn't take Jarrod nearly as long to figure life out as it took me. I admire my son as a human being, and take no credit for any of these amazing qualities of his. Life was hard for him growing up with a crazy man. Although much of our pain manifested differently, I'm sure that we shared a sameness in the intensity of it.

I swore that I would never treat my son the way I was treated, but guess what? In my efforts not to do so, I went totally in the other direction and wound up getting my big ass confronted for it—because both ends of the spectrum were out of balance. Hopefully, when it's Jarrod's turn to be a father, he'll settle somewhere in the middle.

Through all my mistakes, I've presented my son with a lot of AFGEs (Another Frigging Growth Experience), some of which I don't even remember but that I'm quite sure *he* does. In my own defense, never once did I go out and supervise him washing his car . . . then again, I don't think he washes his car. At least I've never seen it shiny and clean like mine. But Jarrod truly doesn't give a shit about appearances (his car always runs well, though).

In spite of the fact that this guy spent much of his young life with a father who was nuts, he had the balls and the magnitude of spirit to hike the entire Appalachian trail. He walked 2,300 miles, from Georgia to Maine, in six months. I don't think I could handle walking to work, which is only 12.2 miles.

Jarrod appears to be comfortable in his skin and is free-spirited and extremely generous. He conducts himself in ways that seem to please him, and that pleases me.

༄ ༄ ༄

Now let's get back to how *I* am so perfect. Little did anyone know that my mother's opinion of me was in part right on the money. I must be somewhat perfect because I continue attracting into my presence these opportunities for joy, and dreams that come true.

A very large part of my present-day joy is my wife, Carin. Originally from New York, Carin's family moved to Arizona when she was eight years old. I wasn't to meet her until 1995, when Miraval opened. She had taken a postion with the resort and from time to time, I would talk with her on the phone as well as drop by her office (so many coincidences, so little time). These chance meetings had to do with my needing to detemine how many people would be in my class each day.

Carin had been employed at Miraval for almost a year before I really had any personal interaction with her. All of the employees were required to attend the various programs at Miraval so they could be able to better explain them to guests.

So, Carin came to the Equine Experience and wanted to work with a 2,000-pound mare named Whitney because she'd first spotted the horse in an employee orientation video I did for the resort and was instantly impressed with her.

Carin's experience during the workshop was quite intense and cathartic, and she later shared with me how deeply affected she was by it. After we worked together, we began to greet each other in a more personal manner, and I found myself noticing that Carin was very attractive. I was also of the opinion that appreciating her beauty from afar was *all* I'd be doing because she was much too young for me.

Just prior to Thanksgiving of 1996, I found out that Carin was about to have a birthday. I still thought she was quite beautiful, and now I was curious about what age she would be turning. So I stopped by her office, and in my most tactful way, I said, "I know that as young as you are you won't mind me asking how old you'll be on your birthday."

She told me, and I thought to myself, *Hell, that's not too young for me at all!*

Then she smiled. Let me just say that then and now it's the prettiest smile I've ever seen. As nervous as I was, I conjured up enough guts to let her know that I was attracted to her. If she didn't feel the same way, I was planning to run as far as I could in the other direction. You see, in spite of all the work I'd done on myself, I could still be a little bit chickenshit, especially when it came to whether or not I was good enough for a pretty woman.

Thankfully, I didn't have to run. We began seeing each other, and to make a long, lovely story short, I began thinking about wanting to marry this woman, which totally shocked me. Prior to meeting her, marriage was the last thing on my mind. I figured I was just going to hang out and have my nice home and my beautiful horses and live happily ever after. And guess what? It wasn't on Carin's mind either. She later told me that she hadn't considered marriage and was quite content living with her dog, Toby. See—my horses didn't trigger me, and her dog didn't trigger her.

Well . . . plans change. About six months into our relationship, I *did* bring up the subject of marriage, and we talked about rings. A ring was not something Carin really wanted, but I truly wanted to give her something as a token of how I felt about her.

I found another way to offer her an engagement gift. I knew she loved Whitney, so I got the horse's ownership papers and signed her over to Carin. I walked up to her, gave her Whitney's papers, and said, "Let this be your ring. Will you marry me?"

She burst into tears and told me that this meant more to her than any ring ever could. We were married a year later, and have now been married for almost four years. One of the things that I've been sharing with people for ages is that in order for relationships to be successful, they have to be a win-win situation. Carin and I are still winners.

After I gave her Whitney, Carin brought me Toby, her chocolate Labrador. God, does Carin love her dog. And since *I* loved *her,* I had to get over my issue with Toby. Of course, the issue wasn't with the dog. He had nothing to do with it. It was about being a wounded little boy. Remember that in my history, dogs had received the nurturing from my father—old "Big Dog" Webb—that I had wanted in my life. Those animals (except for Olive) had never been an integral part of my life, or maybe I was jealous of them. But guess whose job that was to fix? Not Carin's. It was mine.

Toby's not your average, run-of-the-mill dog. He's the most incredible dog I've ever met, and he was determined to get in my pocket. Now, just know that all my life, I've been very much of a neat freak, and I invited into my (formerly immaculate) home a 100-pound dog with brown hair who leaves evidence of his presence all over my light-colored carpet. If anyone ever questions whether or not I love this woman, there's the proof!

But Toby has been an absolute gift to me. We went through a rough patch recently because the vet discovered a small mass, which turned out to be malignant. Toby needed surgery, and we waited to find out if any of the cancer had spread into his bloodstream. Carin was devastated, and to my surprise, so was I.

I cried all day. Couldn't stop. After consulting with the surgeon and with the only veterinary oncologist in Arizona (who just happens to live in Tucson), the recommended course of treatment for Toby was radiation and chemotherapy. It would be extremely expensive, but I was going to do whatever was necessary for Toby. But I was doing this for me, too, because I was getting a huge opportunity to heal my past.

What's amazing about this whole thing is that in the past three months, I've been bombarded with consulting jobs from corporations, which has provided the money to take care of Toby's treatment and then some. Once again, the law of the universe has responded. By the way, Toby is doing great. He's almost completed his chemo and has had no side effects. He comes in every morning with a toy in his mouth and wants to play. Everything about having a dog in the house that I used to dislike no longer exists. I'm just so grateful he's alive. In addition, Carin's happy, and I've healed another wound in my spirit. Life is good.

One of my favorite authors is a man named Anthony DeMello. In his book *Awareness: The Perils and Opportunities of Reality,* he states, "People say they want to be happy. No they don't. They just want relief."

DeMello goes on to say that in order to be happy, people have to wake up. Boy, do I remember the time when all I could think of was just getting some relief. But for the past 22 years, I've been consciously trying to wake up. I'm so glad that I was at least awake enough to see Carin and the gifts our relationship brings to us both every single day.

We're on this path together. She doesn't want to be asleep either. Is this easy? Hell, no. Is it more than I ever thought possible? Hell, yes. For instance, I never would have thought in a million years that I could come close to having 50,000 words to put down on paper . . .

or that anyone would be interested in having me do it.

Everything that you've read in this book was totally necessary to bring me to this point, and I haven't even scratched the surface as to what is possible. Every pain, every feeling of shame, every terrifying moment, and all the misery I inflicted on others and the guilt that went with it was all necessary, it seems.

It's so true that we live in a universe of duality. I spent the first half of my life doing everything I could to find out what life is *not,* and now I think I'm beginning, ever so slightly, to get little hints of what it *is*. And when I'm there, I'm in joy. When I'm in self-doubt and fear, I'm in deep shit once again.

I hope that what you've read here has been helpful to you. I really thank you for reading this, and I hope that someday we'll meet personally, hang out with the horses, explore what doesn't work, and discover how we could do things differently.

My name is still Wyatt, and I'm 58 years old. I went to bed last night knowing that God isn't pissed off at me.

In fact, He loves me very much and is a friend of mine.

∽ ∽ ∽ ∽ ∽ ∽

About Wyatt Webb

W^ho is Wyatt Webb? He's a native of a 250-person town in rural Georgia who survived 15 years in the music industry as an entertainer, touring the country 30 weeks a year. Realizing he was practically killing himself due to drug and alcohol addiction, Wyatt sought help, which eventually led him to quit the entertainment industry. He began what is now a 20-year career as a therapist. A job at his original rehab center in Nashville, Tennessee, evolved into his becoming the head of an adolescent treatment program at Arizona's famed Sierra Tucson facility. Eventually, Wyatt would become one of the most creative, unconventional, and sought-after therapists in the country. Today he's the founder and leader of the Equine Experience at Miraval, one of the world's top resorts, which is also located in Tucson.

If you would like to learn more about Wyatt Webb's Equine Experience programs held throughout the year at Miraval, please call: (800) 232-3969.

About Cindy Pearlman

Cindy Pearlman is a nationally syndicated writer for the *New York Times Syndicate* and the *Chicago Sun-Times*. Her work has appeared in *Entertainment Weekly, Premiere, People, Ladies' Home Journal, McCall's, Seventeen, Movieline,* and *Cinescape*. Over the past 15 years, she has interviewed Hollywood's biggest stars, who appear in her column "The Big Picture." Cindy is also the co-author, along with Jim Brickman, of *Simple Things*.

✑ ✑ ✑

We hope you enjoyed this Hay House book. If you would
like to receive a free catalog featuring additional Hay House
books and products, or if you would like information about
the Hay Foundation, please contact:

Hay House, Inc.
P.O. Box 5100
Carlsbad, CA 92018-5100

(760) **431-7695** or (800) **654-5126**
(760) **431-6948 (fax)** or (800) **650-5115 (fax)**
www.hayhouse.com® • **www.hayfoundation.org**

✑ ✑ ✑

Published and distributed in Australia by: Hay House Australia Pty.
Ltd., 18/36 Ralph St., Alexandria NSW 2015 • *Phone:* 612-9669-4299
• *Fax:* 612-9669-4144 • www.hayhouse.com.au

Published and distributed in the United Kingdom by: Hay House UK,
Ltd., 292B Kensal Rd., London W10 5BE • *Phone:* 44-20-8962-1230 •
Fax: 44-20-8962-1239 • www.hayhouse.co.uk

Published and distributed in the Republic of South Africa by: Hay
House SA (Pty), Ltd., P.O. Box 990, Witkoppen 2068 • *Phone/Fax:* 27-
11-467-8904 • orders@psdprom.co.za • www.hayhouse.co.za

Published in India by: Hay House Publishers India, Muskaan Complex,
Plot No. 3, B-2, Vasant Kunj, New Delhi 110 070 • *Phone:* 91-11-
4176-1620 • *Fax:* 91-11-4176-1630 • www.hayhouse.co.in

Distributed in Canada by: Raincoast, 9050 Shaughnessy St.,
Vancouver, B.C. V6P 6E5 • *Phone:* (604) 323-7100 •
Fax: (604) 323-2600 • www.raincoast.com

✑ ✑ ✑

Tune in to **HayHouseRadio.com®** for the best in inspirational talk radio
featuring top Hay House authors! And, sign up via the Hay House USA
Website to receive the Hay House online newsletter and stay informed about
what's going on with your favorite authors. You'll receive bimonthly
announcements about Discounts and Offers, Special Events, Product
Highlights, Free Excerpts, Giveaways, and more!
www.hayhouse.com®